New Monetarism

by

David Roche and Bob McKee

ISBN 978-1-4357-0088-8

The authors

David Roche is President and chief global strategist of Independent Strategy, a global investment consultancy based in London, Hong Kong and Zurich. He has worked in the investment business for over 30 years and was formerly global strategist for Morgan Stanley before founding Independent Strategy. He has been particularly acclaimed for predicting the Fall of the Wall and the end of the Soviet era in the 1980s; the emergence of global disinflation in 1990s with purchasing power going from corporations to the people; and for forecasting the Asian financial crash of 1997-8. Irish by birth, he lives in Hong Kong.

Bob McKee is chief economist at Independent Strategy. He has also worked in the investment business for decades and was formerly part of David Roche's global strategy team at Morgan Stanley. Like David, he is a regular contributor to business broadcasting including TV with CNBC, BBC, Bloomberg etc as well as for various printed journals. He is British and lives in London.

Contents

The prologue

As we go to press in September 2007, financial markets around the world have experienced a significant fall in prices. The drop had its origin in a liquidity crunch driven by falling risk appetite, a rising cost of capital and a reversal of the yen carry trade — just the factors predicted in the arguments of New Monetarism.

As we expected, it was not a decline in any of the indicators of traditional monetary aggregates like M3 money supply that revealed the crunch. No, investors had to look at the indicators of New Monetarism, such as the spreads on exotic new liquidity instruments like credit default swaps or collateralised debt obligations.

We think this makes the story we tell in the following pages even more pertinent to investors.

The great serendipity

Liquidity may be the most overused word in the financial lexicon but it is among the most meaningful for asset prices. No one watching the electric action of financial markets in spring and summer 2007 can have any doubt that, when the quantity and cost of money available for investment changes or when risk appetite to lend or borrow it shifts, asset markets can freeze to the point of threatening the global financial system.

This short book tells how and why this happens. It defines 'liquidity' and describes how its changing nature in recent decades makes it a more vital concept for investors than the so-called 'real' economy that produces all the goods and services we use in our daily lives. We shall share with you the tools we use to match investment strategy with the liquidity cycle.

In the old days the economic cycle set the tone of financial markets. Now with global financial assets valued at about 8-10 times GDP, the current of causality runs the other way. As often as not, financial markets set the tone of the real economy. How this came to be and how it works are captured by our theory of New Monetarism.

New Monetarism describes a set of economic conditions that for two decades allowed for the creation of massive liquidity without engendering high inflation in goods and services or a high cost of capital. Instead, the value of financial assets grew far faster than the underlying economy.

Why this happened was this. From the early 1980s sane central bank policies, globalisation and technologies such as the internet allied to reduce inflation progressively. Lower inflation meant cheap money. Lots of it was created and in many new forms, most dedicated to investing rather than shopping. Because of this, and the new supply of cheap goods and services over the internet and from China, increased liquidity did not result in inflation in the shops, but in asset prices.

INTRODUCTION

At the same time, lower inflation put a stop to 'stop-go' economic cycles. Economies went on expanding steadily for very long periods of time. As a result, the 'volatility' of the macro economy fell. This meant that growth; jobs, wages and profits were also much less volatile than before. This phenomenon is known as The Great Moderation. All of these factors together are the great serendipity that allowed New Monetarism to exist. New Monetarism is not so much a new paradigm as the result of propitious economic circumstances and thus will last for only as long as they do.

Is New Monetarism good or bad news for the world economy and people's wealth? Liquidity like beauty can be virtuous or evil. On the one hand, the world needs liquidity to make the wheels of wealth and of the global economy rotate. Too little and the wheels will grind to a halt.

The new forms of liquidity under New Monetarism have increased the shock absorption capacity of markets by decreasing financial market volatility and spreading financial risk better. They have provided a new insurance function against changes in interest rates or default in traditional debt markets.

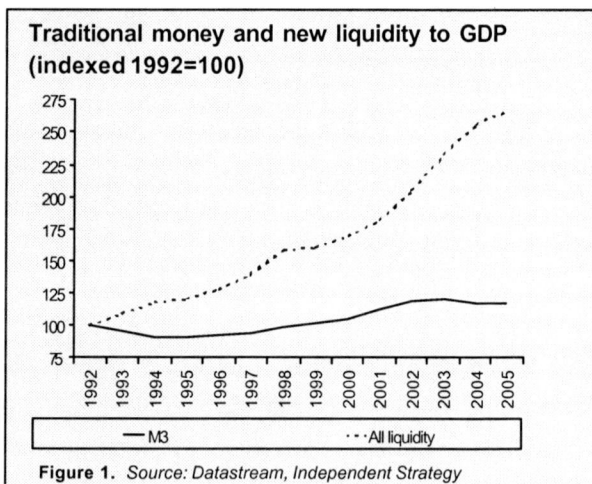

Figure 1. *Source: Datastream, Independent Strategy*

That contributed to increased confidence and lower volatility in asset prices. Banks and corporations thus felt comfortable in increasing the lending and leverage relative to reserves and equity.

INTRODUCTION

But the positive impacts of such financial engineering (risk absorption capacity) can also encourage excessive risk taking, lending and borrowing based on 'flat world' faith. Flat world faith is a sense of false confidence that the superlative financial engineering of New Monetarism has ended economic and financial cycles.

This faith affects human behaviour. If a businessman believes that profits and the cost of money will never change, he will borrow and invest more than if he is uncertain about these factors in the future. This confidence opens the way for high levels of liquidity creation (the fruit of excess borrowing and lending). But it also means severe liquidity contraction, when all is reversed.

For that to happen, the quantity of liquidity has to shrink or its price has to rise or the willingness to lend and borrow has to fall. That is what is starting to happen now in global financial markets. And because financial assets and wealth are now valued so much more than the real economy, the spill-over effect will be felt in the global economy soon.

For this, do not blame New Monetarism or the financial engineering of new financial markets. It is down to how people use these financial instruments. To map how to cope with this uncertain future and protect wealth is the purpose of this book.

And if you want a more light-hearted look at how New Monetarism has worked for good and ill, read our final chapter on the story of Coconut Island.

CHAPTER ONE

New Monetarism and disinflation

Our story starts with the last 25 years of disinflation. What is disinflation? It is years of falling price increases, but not (in a generalised sense) falling prices. That would be deflation, not disinflation.

From about 1982, global price increases slowed year after year. This disinflation was caused by several factors.

First, sane central bankers started to target low inflation as a priority for monetary policy. Second, globalisation empowered producers of cheap things, like China, to sell their wares to rich folk without too much interference from protectionist tariffs or quotas.

Third, the internet created competition in consumer markets and so shifted pricing power away from producers to the people.

Fourth, the internet also made it easier for companies to manage global supply chains more efficiently.

And finally, governments acted to empower markets rather than strangle them and also limit their own spending and deficits.

Most of the improvement in inflation came early in the disinflationary period (Figure 2). Thereafter, inflation marked time, but at a sustained low level.

Figure 2. *Source: Datastream, Independent Strategy*

NEW MONETARISM AND DISINFLATION

In the 1980s, the battle against inflation was fought (and won) by central bankers. So beating inflation was a monetary phenomenon.

Only subsequently in the 1990s did Chinese production and the spread of the internet keep prices low.

Indeed, at first, the bond market didn't believe that inflation was licked for a very long time after it was. That's because inflationary expectations had been set by monetary and fiscal policies in the first 25 years after the second world war. So investors were reluctant to buy bonds in the early years of disinflation because they just didn't believe that lower inflation would last.

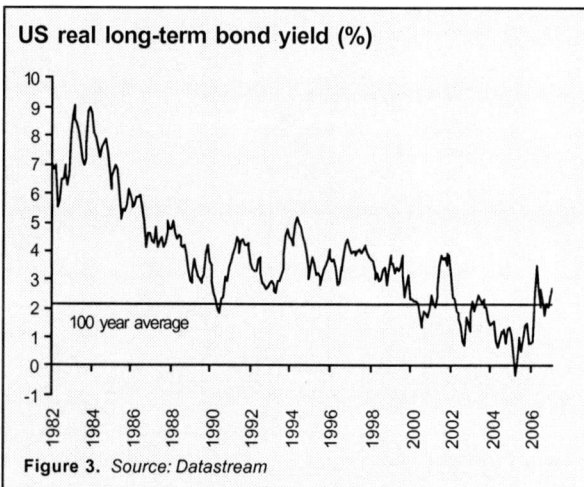

US real long-term bond yield (%)

100 year average

Figure 3. *Source: Datastream*

As a result, bond yields stayed high in real terms (after inflation is deducted) and declined only gradually as investor expectations adjusted to the new disinflationary world.

By the time the disinflationary period ended around 2001 the real cost of long-term debt was way below its long-term average (Figure 3), or what could be considered the 'natural rate' that equates supply of capital with productive investment.

Inflation began to return to the global economy since 2001, if only moderately. But bond markets still seem to expect inflation to be low forever and real yields remain low historically. Perhaps this represents the same lag in the adjustment of inflationary expectations to underlying reality as at the beginning of the disinflationary decades, but now operating in reverse.

Disinflation's double whammy

Disinflation made us all rich. All asset prices rose in relation to their income. That's because disinflation gave us lower inflation and a lower real cost of capital. The combination made every dollar earned in the future worth more today.

So capitalisation rates rose: the value of every asset, from houses to equities, rose faster than the income each could (potentially) generate. Viewed another way, familiar to equity investors, the asset price multiple (think of it as sort of a giant P/E of the whole economy), judged by the value of capital used to produce all output, jumped up in a step change.

Disinflation also helped corporate managers to make higher profits by keeping wage costs (under pressure from China's 'boundless' cheap labour) down. Lower inflation also meant corporations could make better long-term investment decisions. After all, how long is your investment horizon if inflation is 100% or higher, making all profits worthless after a year?

So, during the disinflationary decades, corporations saw the E in P/E grow fast, while the P was expanding even faster. That is the secret of disinflation's double wealth whammy. It boosted income. But it also hefted the present value or price that investors were willing to pay to get that income.

Effect of disinflation on average nominal equity return (% p.a.)

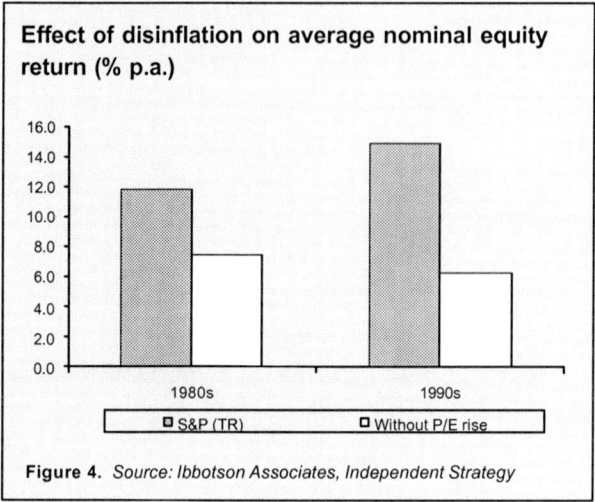

Figure 4. *Source: Ibbotson Associates, Independent Strategy*

Of the two wealth effects, the biggest was the effect of lower inflation and higher capitalisation rates on asset prices. For US equities, during the disinflationary decades, rising P/Es accounted for two-thirds of total returns in equity markets and rising corporate profits only one-third (Figure 4).

Moreover, the price of 'unproductive' real estate rose even more relative to rent than the price of equity in the (presumably) 'productive' corporate sector increased relative to profits.

So people got wealthier from rising asset values. And they got wealthier way faster than from rising GDP, profits or rents (Figure 5).

G7 financial assets (money, bonds, equities) as % of GDP

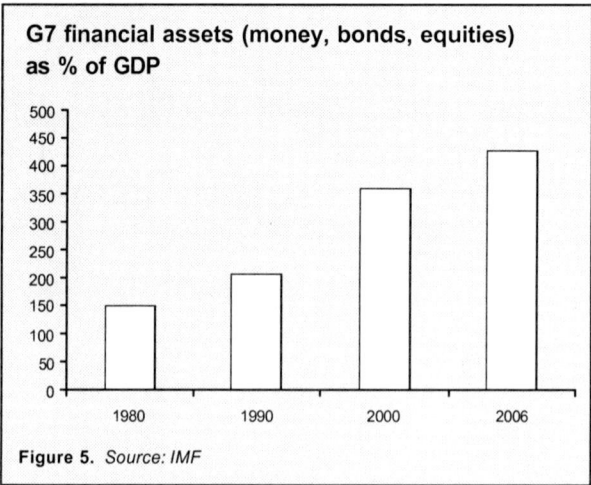

Figure 5. *Source: IMF*

But wealth can grow faster than GDP only if some or all of three things are in place.

First, the share of profits (the income assets earn) in GDP must expand. It did throughout the disinflationary years because the wage share was compressed (Figure 6).

This didn't make workers too unhappy because wages were also growing (albeit not as fast as GDP) and the globalisation of trade was making things cheaper for workers to buy. So workers got richer in real terms, if not as quickly as the owners (although they were increasingly the same people through participation in pension funds, retirement accounts, mutual funds etc).

Wealth can also grow faster than GDP if inflation shifts permanently to a lower plane and/or (often as a result) the cost of capital does. As we described above, this boosts asset values relative to income or GDP (national income).

And finally, wealth can rise faster than GDP if there is enough of the right type of money around to fund rising asset values and output without driving up inflation for goods and services.

New Monetarism enters stage left!

This is where New Monetarism enters the stage. This was the other major reason why, during disinflation, financial assets grew much more in value than GDP or than any 'material' economic activity underpinning asset values.

Rising financial asset prices was partly the result of the better mobilisation of existing credit and equity markets (i.e.

Peaks in US domestic corporate profit cycle (% share of GDP)

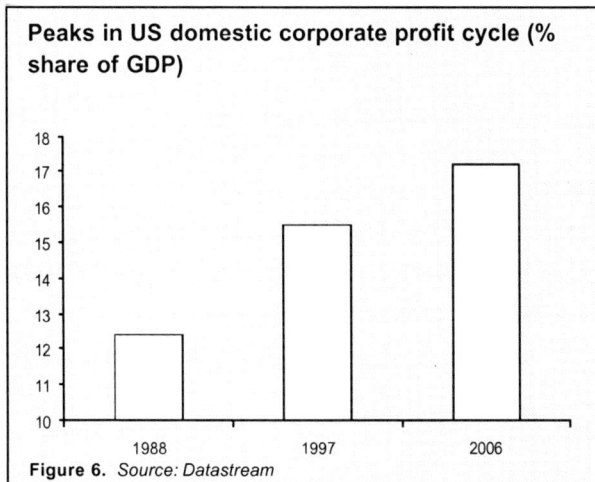

Figure 6. *Source: Datastream*

How money multiplies — the old and the new monetarism

OLD SYSTEM	NEW MONETARISM
Central bank power money	Central bank power money
Credit multiplier	Credit multiplier / Global ATMs (carry trade; US CA deficit) / Risk appetite (derivative markets; low volatility)
	Leverage
Total domestic liquidity	Total global liquidity

Figure 7. *Source: Independent Strategy*

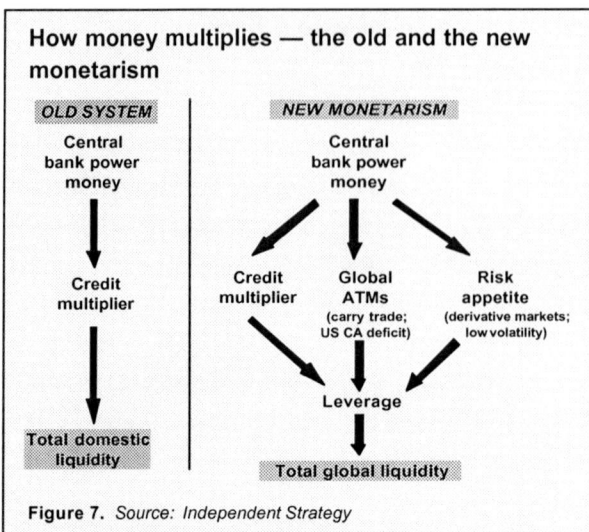

financial market liberalisation). But we contend that the biggest factor was the creation of new financial instruments.

A new form of liquidity (i.e. money) was being created outside the central bankers' control (Figure 7). And this 'liquidity' was in excess of the needs of the 'real economy' to create more GDP and instead pumped up asset prices.

Some would deny this as an explanation of rising asset values. What about the impact of increased labour productivity during the disinflation decades? Surely, that justifies higher asset values?

But much of the expansion in liquidity is not commensurate with the great boosts to productivity we are told about. Yes, labour got more productive under disinflation, but what about capital productivity?

When measuring capital expenditure in GDP, economists usually count only investment in equipment, buildings and factories (in some countries, software has recently been added). So GDP accounting, and therefore productivity measurement, ignores most investment that occurs in creating brand names and goodwill among customers, in training people, or in streamlining or structuring organisations to prosper in the globalised economy, and in shuffling assets (accounting and investment).

Excluding these sorts of investment expenditures in the definition of capital formation is anachronistic and Dickensian. It says if you can't kick it, it isn't an investment. But the rich countries of the world are now predominantly service economies. Much of their investments cannot be kicked. One recent study that tried to measure investment in intangibles that you can't kick found that the true level of investment in the US was 60-70% above the official figures.

Conventional GDP accounting treats most of these 'intangible' assets as either costs (leading to the understatement of both profits and assets), or as transfers (in which case, GDP accounting doesn't include them at all). But if you add in intangible investments, then the productivity of capital is much lower and partly explains why the growth of liquidity has outstripped that of GDP in the last 20 years.

All this 'intangible' investment occurs within the corporate sector. So old GDP accounting means that business expenses are being overstated and profit and capital formation are being understated by the amount of 'intangible' investment. But the result is that, by increasing the amount of assets relative to GDP, capital productivity is reduced. In sum, we may be using more capital than we think and getting less productivity than we account for by the usual measurements.

New forms of liquidity

But what are these new forms of liquidity that constitute the foundation of New Monetarism?

In the good old days of the 1960s and 1970s, central bankers set the supply and price of money. They issued 'power money', then the banks borrowed it and lent it, keeping some in reserve. And the sum of the whole thing (power money and bank lending) was liquidity measured traditionally as 'broad money'.

NEW MONETARISM AND DISINFLATION

Sure, there was also securitised debt, but this was nearly all government borrowing, at least outside the US. For this was in the days when Germans couldn't have credit cards and Koreans couldn't get mortgages.

As disinflation multiplied the value of financial assets, central banks progressively lost control of money. Financial players, increasingly sure of cheap money, began to introduce new-fangled financial instruments that created liquidity independently of the central bank. So central bank power money became a smaller and smaller part of total debt and broad money (Figure 8).

All this new money didn't boost officially-measured inflation because globalisation and technology kept down the prices of most things we buy rather than invest in. This was particularly true for the prices of manufactured products that bore the brunt of the increased competition from globalisation.

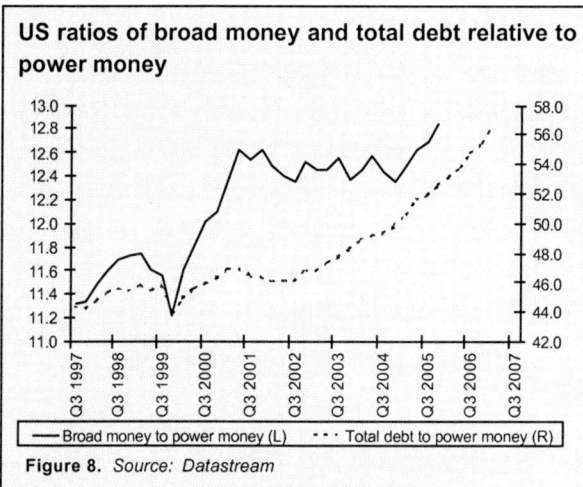

US ratios of broad money and total debt relative to power money

Figure 8. Source: Datastream

In contrast, the price of assets began to soar, as money got cheaper and more plentiful. But no one counts asset price inflation as inflation. Indeed, asset price inflation is always called wealth creation until the credit bubble of underpriced capital that always lies at its base finally bursts.

New forms of securitised debt sprang up: mortgage debt, corporate debt and other asset-backed debt. But the most important new form of liquidity was through the development of derivatives.

Derivatives: a hedge against risk or a credit Titanic?

Are derivatives merely a form of 'neutral' transactional capital that increases the depth of financial markets without adding to risk or influencing asset prices? Or do they raise the risk of financial instability and collapse? The answer will help decide whether derivatives are for good or evil in our modern financial world.

The answer, of course, is both. Derivatives are not only transactional capital, but also a form of liquidity that influences asset prices. Metaphorically, derivatives are to financial liquidity what tilting the basin is to water — they increase the sloshing in whatever direction the market is leaning: bullish or bearish.

In a long-running bull market, derivatives create multiple means for more players to invest in more assets in a more leveraged fashion. This increases the 'investment power' (purchasing power) of money. It is pretty obvious that if one can buy a security that represents 100% of an asset for 3-5% of the value of the asset, then an awful lot of liquidity has been freed up in relation to the underlying assets.

So, in their simplest form, many derivatives allow an investor to participate in 100% of the change in income or price of an underling asset for a fraction of its cost.

A nice image is that of a real estate derivative where an investor can buy or sell any change in the future value or rent of a shop or house at a fraction of its cost provided he accepts the greater risk of the derivative instrument. This increases market liquidity is because buying the derivative is cheaper than buying the house. Unless demand for property has negative price elasticity the cheaper alternative — the derivative —

US commercial banks' derivative contracts by type ($trn)

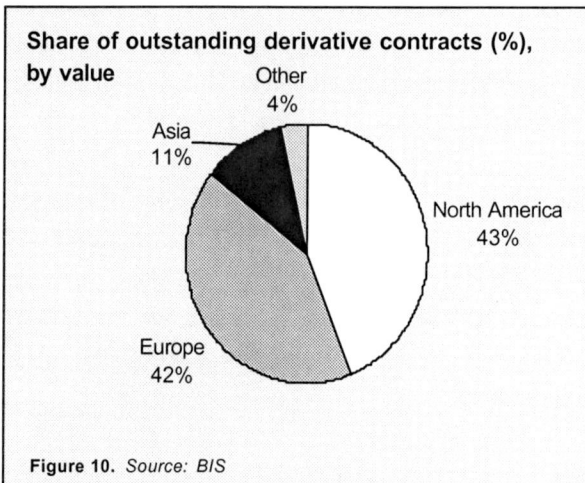

Figure 9. *Source: US Comptroller of the Currency*

Share of outstanding derivative contracts (%), by value

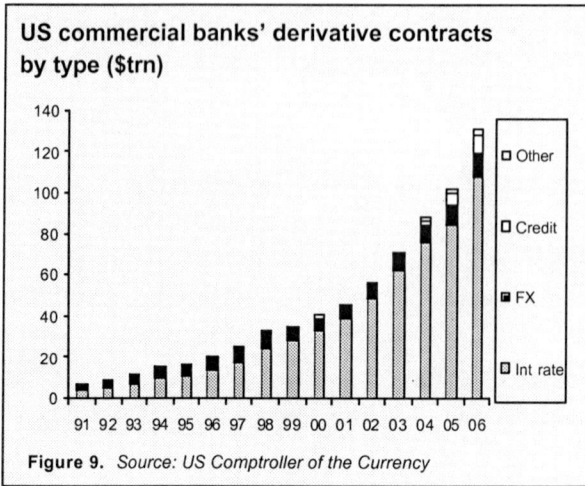

Other 4%
Asia 11%
North America 43%
Europe 42%

Figure 10. *Source: BIS*

will attract new players to the property market. That is how liquidity is created.

Derivative contracts are mainly based on bets on interest rates (Figure 9), although there has been a sharp increase in more exotic derivative instruments in recent years based on foreign exchange, equities, credit defaults and real estate.

Most derivatives are linked to assets in the US and Europe not in Asia (Figure 10). This is not a coincidence, but because the US and Europe are the places in the world with the fastest rising asset prices. This is where the most 'asset pricing money' was created.

In contrast, after the bursting of the Japanese stock bubble in 1989 and the Asian currency crises of 1997-8, financial institutions in Asia were preoccupied with the need to shrink their balance sheets, rather than pump them up using derivatives to do so.

NEW MONETARISM AND DISINFLATION

As the vast majority of derivatives concern interest rates (e.g. swaps) or credit defaults (e.g. CDS), they are mostly used to transfer interest rate or default risk of a loan or bond off a bank's balance sheet to others like specialised hedge funds or insurance companies (Figure 11).

Or derivatives can be used to fix the return or cost of an asset or liability by transferring the interest rate risk to another party. Thus, as in the case of securitised debt, derivatives free up credit capacity by spreading risk.

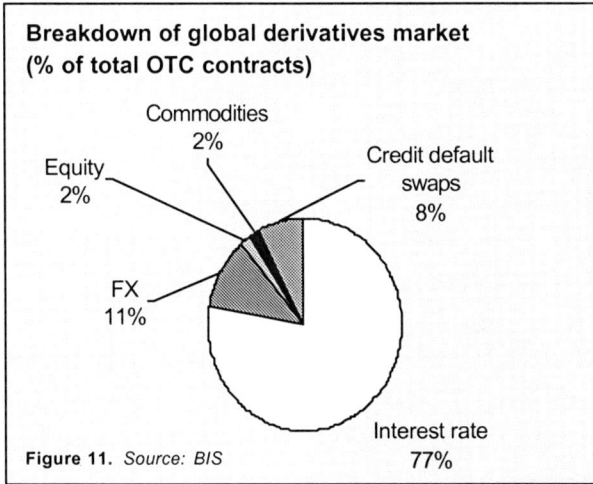

Breakdown of global derivatives market (% of total OTC contracts)

Commodities 2%

Credit default swaps 8%

Equity 2%

FX 11%

Interest rate 77%

Figure 11. *Source: BIS*

By spreading risk and increasing the shock absorption capacity of markets, derivatives contribute to reducing the volatility of financial assets, along with many macroeconomic variables such as growth in GDP, wages, profits and inflation.

This creates widespread confidence that a low volatility world, characterised by contained inflation, low interest rates and a fairly flat, predictable and manageable economic cycle, will become a durable feature of the future. It is understandable that investors will want to take on more leverage than would otherwise be the case. This too generates liquidity. It is also why the notional value of derivatives dwarfs the underlying assets they represent.

Derivatives are an integral part of the investment universe for leveraged players such as hedge funds and private equity firms. Derivatives are used to lock-in the cost of debt in private equity firms that leverage to boost the returns of the corporate assets they invest in.

NEW MONETARISM AND DISINFLATION

Derivatives sell risk off financial institutions' balance sheets to institutions which may be better able to bear it because they are more numerous or more specialised in doing so.

If this is right, then derivatives may also have improved the structure of the watertight bulkheads on the good ship of finance. So, if an iceberg of financial crisis should puncture one compartment, it won't sink the financial ship.

In the very recent past, bubbles have burst without causing a generalised financial market crash — US equities in 2000, bankruptcies like Refco and LTCM, Aussie and UK housing in 2004, US housing and a bucket of Middle-Eastern equity markets in 2006).

No wonder bank regulators take the view that derivatives are basically good news. So they allow the banks to create more loans to replace those for which derivatives have taken the risk off the balance sheet, although the banks must continue to provide for counter party risk. This adds to credit growth. In other words, the regulators believe that, although derivatives make the vessel of liquidity bigger, they make it safer and less volatile.

As a result, in the US, the value of derivative contracts held by the five major US banks have been allowed to rise to 350% of their risk capital and also make up nearly 100% of capital for the top 25 US banks (Figure 12).

However, it is our contention that the bank regulators are ignoring the 'evil' side of the derivatives explosion. For if derivatives are a form of underpriced liquidity that create asset bubbles, then the impact of any bursting of these credit bubbles will become magnified by the size of any losses in the derivative markets.

Thus a 10% loss on an underlying asset can be magnified into a 100% loss on the derivative contract. The damage would then be inflicted on the real economy through contraction of credit by the damaged financial sector.

Total derivatives credit exposure to capital ratio (%) of US banks

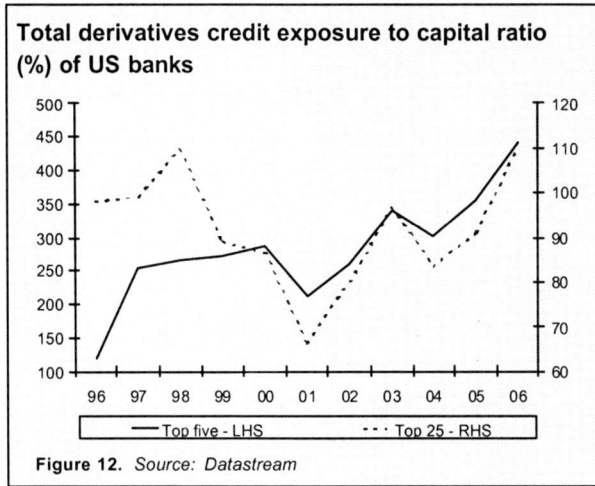

Figure 12. *Source: Datastream*

This is where the story gets darker.

CHAPTER TWO

The Liquidity Pyramid

Our measurement of liquidity is not that of an economist. It encompasses variables that provide evidence of risk appetite, credit multipliers and the quantity of money and sums them all into a Liquidity Pyramid. The pyramid is a symbol and expression of the supply and demand for liquidity.

We define liquidity *as any form of money that can be used to: buy goods or services; or invest in an asset in order to freeze the cost of (or the return on) holding an asset or liability; or in order to transfer the risk to another party.*

Today global liquidity is like a massive pyramid standing on its head (Figure 13). It represents at least ten years of GDP and is growing at least five times faster than GDP.

At the bottom of this inverted pyramid is a tiny triangle of central bank power money. This supports and expands into broad money. That, plus a

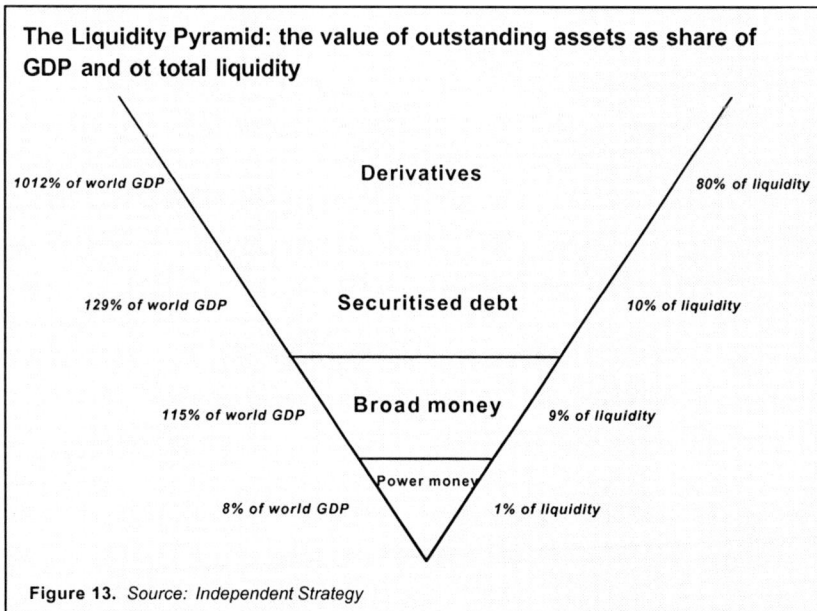

The Liquidity Pyramid: the value of outstanding assets as share of GDP and ot total liquidity

1012% of world GDP	Derivatives	80% of liquidity
129% of world GDP	Securitised debt	10% of liquidity
115% of world GDP	Broad money	9% of liquidity
8% of world GDP	Power money	1% of liquidity

Figure 13. *Source: Independent Strategy*

few minor add-ons, was the sum total of liquidity when we were starting our financial services career nearly 40 years ago.

On top of broad money now comes a much bigger slice of the liquidity pyramid, composed of securitised debt markets, where much traditional bank lending now gets sold off as bonds.

Finally, at the top come the massive derivative and other exotic asset markets, comprising nearly 75% of total global liquidity.

These different tranches of the pyramid represent different types of liquidity. Like medieval cities with their own monies that could only be used within their walled confines, New Monetarism has created different monies for different areas of activity.

But the walls between each of these categories of money are not watertight and there are spillovers. For example, overdrafts and margin accounts can bridge different categories of money. Another spillover is when rising asset prices lead to more household wealth, which in turn enables consumer spending to increase.

Using either power money (notes and coins) or broad money (your cheque book or credit card) you can do your weekly supermarket run and even buy your car. With securitised debt (which is what your home loan will become in nano seconds of the bank making it) you can buy a house or you can borrow to invest. But with derivatives you can invest only in financial assets and commodities.

The biggest, fastest growing slug of liquidity (derivatives) is destined for buying financial assets, not shopping for things and services. No wonder the price of the former soared and the price of the latter disinflated!

The liquidity pyramid is growing like wildfire. Between 1990 and 2005 in the US, it expanded by 300% while GDP grew only 80% (Figure 14).

THE LIQUIDITY PYRAMID

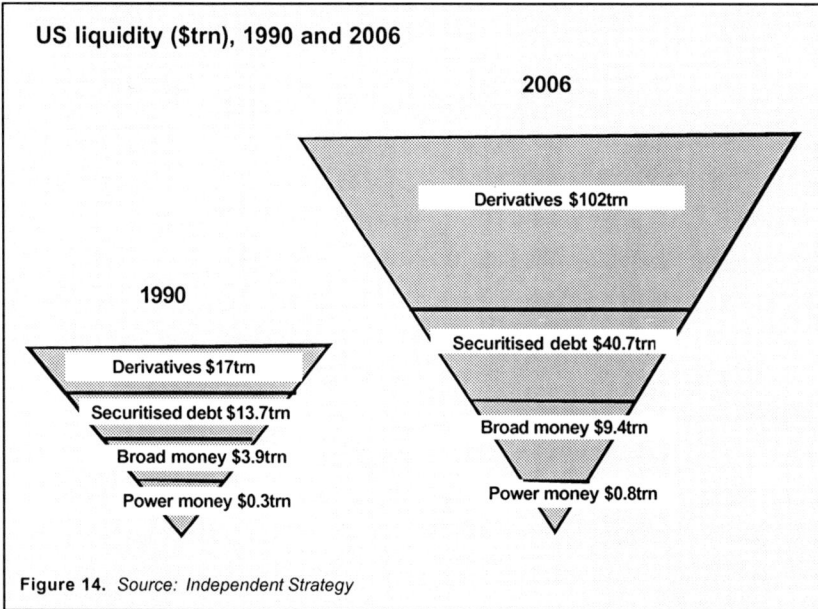

US liquidity ($trn), 1990 and 2006

2006

Derivatives $102trn

1990

Derivatives $17trn

Securitised debt $13.7trn

Broad money $3.9trn

Power money $0.3trn

Securitised debt $40.7trn

Broad money $9.4trn

Power money $0.8trn

Figure 14. *Source: Independent Strategy*

Securitised debt alone grew by a factor by 200%. So the liquidity to buy financial assets grew twice as fast as the money to shop (Figure 15).

Excess liquidity growth over and above nominal GDP growth has been much faster

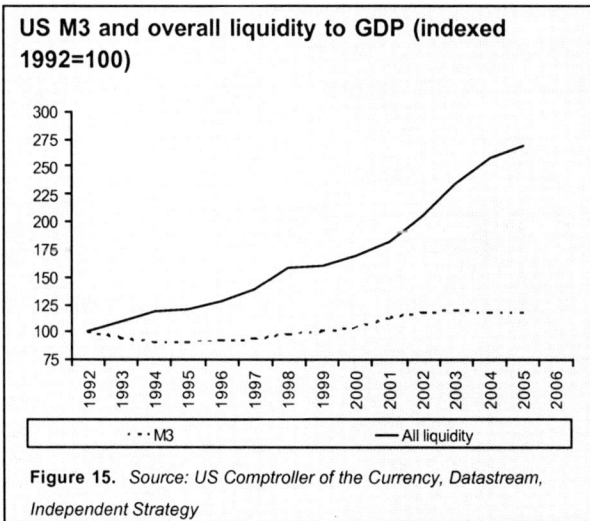

US M3 and overall liquidity to GDP (indexed 1992=100)

··· M3 —— All liquidity

Figure 15. *Source: US Comptroller of the Currency, Datastream, Independent Strategy*

than central bankers dare admit. But the compartmentalisation of this liquidity has stopped it generating faster generalised inflation of goods and services.

THE LIQUIDITY PYRAMID

How underpriced capital became the US's most successful export

What is happening in the US applies to the globe. In Europe, the duplication of the US liquidity pyramid is almost complete. But the way in which the US transmits its model to the world is not limited to other countries emulating its monetary architecture. There are two other transmission mechanisms that make New Monetarism the US's most successful export.

One is that, as 'wealth' is created, it boosts consumption. Part of the additional 'wealth' is turned into shopping money (through selling assets, home equity withdrawals or other forms of increased borrowing). Rising asset values also mean that consumers save less from their incomes because their assets do their saving for them simply by increasing in value. As they get richer, consumers feel more confident and shopping is fun.

This is true everywhere. But in the case of the US, excessive consumer expenditure means that the country spends more than it produces and this creates a current account deficit equal to its savings shortfall (Figure 16).

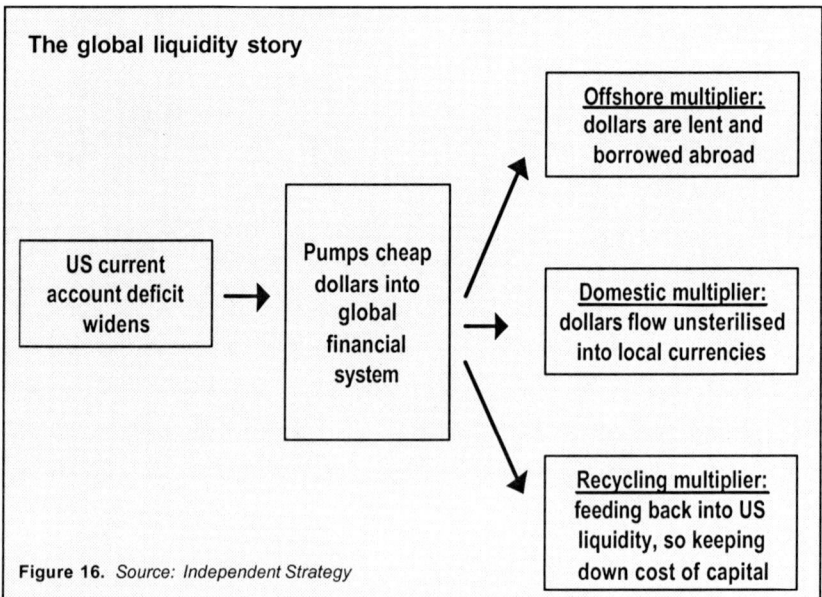

The global liquidity story

US current account deficit widens → Pumps cheap dollars into global financial system →

Offshore multiplier: dollars are lent and borrowed abroad

Domestic multiplier: dollars flow unsterilised into local currencies

Recycling multiplier: feeding back into US liquidity, so keeping down cost of capital

Figure 16. *Source: Independent Strategy*

THE LIQUIDITY PYRAMID

A current account deficit means that dollars created by the liquidity pyramid, which get spent on excess consumption, get sent abroad to pay for imports and are left in the hands of foreigners. Some of those dollars never return home and end up in foreign monetary systems and in offshore banks. There they may be lent and borrowed many times over so that each dollar can get multiplied into more than one.

Some dollars get changed into local currency in countries running an external surplus with the US. Those dollars, converted into local currency, are deposited in local banks. If the local currency equivalent of the dollar inflow is not borrowed by the central bank (i.e. sterilised), once again the credit multiplier goes to work.

Those dollars that are changed into local currency end up in the central bank. The central bank (or finance ministry in some Asian countries) recycles them back to the US. There they are invested in fixed income securities, so sustaining or adding to, the US credit pyramid.

So at the end of the day — or, more precisely, when the global credit multiplier is done — one little dollar repeats the miracle of the loaves and fishes.

The story of how the US influences global liquidity doesn't stop there. In recent years, wealth creation and expanding consumption made the US the fastest-growing economy in the world. As a result, Fed policy became global monetary policy to a significant extent.

Because other major economies (Japan and Europe) were much weaker than the US, they couldn't afford to let their currencies strengthen against the dollar. To do so would have damaged their exports and boosted their imports, hitting their own output and jobs.

So, they had to operate a closet dollar-peg currency system, keeping their currencies in line with the US on foreign exchanges. The only way to do that was to keep their currencies cheap and mirror low US interest rates.

THE LIQUIDITY PYRAMID

Net long contracts ('000s) in ¥/$ at the CME and ¥/$ exchange rate

Figure 17. *Source: Datastream*

Yen real effective exchange rate index (1973=100)

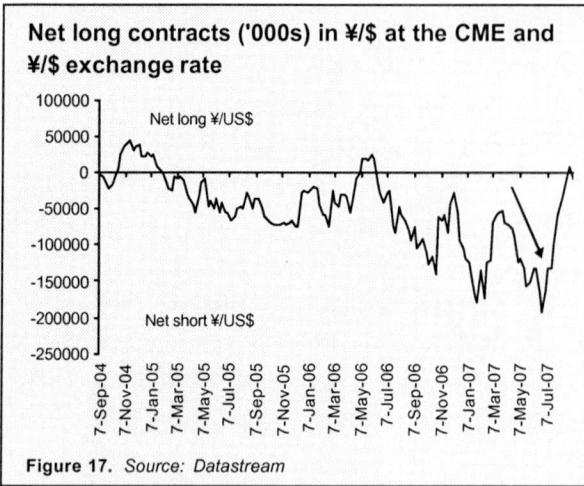

Figure 18. *Source: Datastream*

The rest followed. Cheap money allowed many of their financial markets to run riot, creating the liquidity pyramid that inflated asset prices just as in the US.

Japan: the alternative global ATM: free cash on demand

It would be wrong to attribute all growth in international liquidity to the US. Nor is a *current account* deficit the only way to do so. Japan is a big contributor to global liquidity through its *capital* account deficit.

Capital is abnormally cheaply priced in Japan. But in Japan's case this is to combat deflation and facilitate restructuring, particularly in the banking sector. This encouraged Japanese investors to pour funds into higher-yielding assets abroad. At one point, Japanese housewives owned nearly half of New Zealand's bond market!

Non-Japanese investors have also been borrowing cheap yen to buy higher-yielding foreign assets too (Figure 17). This operation is called the Great Carry Trade (see Inset 1 on page 22). As a result, the yen became the most undervalued major currency in the world (Figure 18).

The carry trade

Everyone in Japan has benefited from a weak yen. The major short yen players onshore in Japan have been households and Japanese banks. Households (through investment trusts) have quintupled their exposure to high-yielding foreign assets, though they are still less than 3% of household financial assets. Also, household foreign investment exposure in counted in yen. The yen has been very weak. So part of the build-up in Japanese household assets is not a flow but simply a currency revaluation effect.

Japan's balance of payments tells just part of the story. Japan runs a large current account surplus. FDI outflows are much smaller, if growing. Yet its international

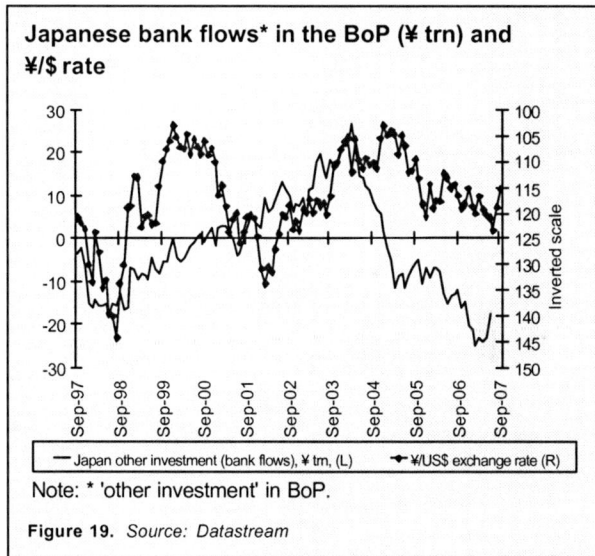

Japanese bank flows* in the BoP (¥ trn) and ¥/$ rate

— Japan other investment (bank flows), ¥ trn, (L)   ← ¥/US$ exchange rate (R)

Note: * 'other investment' in BoP.

Figure 19. *Source: Datastream*

reserves have virtually stopped rising. So capital is being recycled abroad by households and banks, not by little green men from Mars.

The Japanese financial institutions are lending heavily abroad (Figure 19). Outside the banks, Japanese investment institutions are all very, very long foreign assets.

THE LIQUIDITY PYRAMID

Sources of yen carry trade

Chart A: Japan — investment trusts, foreign currency assets (¥trn)

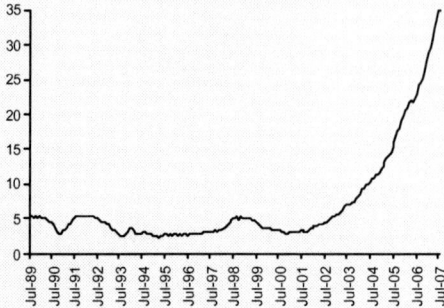

What are the sources of the yen carry trade and how big is it? The main sources include Japanese citizens who have conducted a form of the carry trade in seeking higher yield by investing in foreign assets. This is revealed in the increase in Japanese holdings of foreign assets held through investment trusts, which citizens have been able to buy through the post office since 2005. This comes to about ¥7trn annually, or $60bn, accumulating to ¥30trn by the end of 2005 (Chart A).

Chart B: Share of Japanese household financial assets in foreign-denominated investments (%)

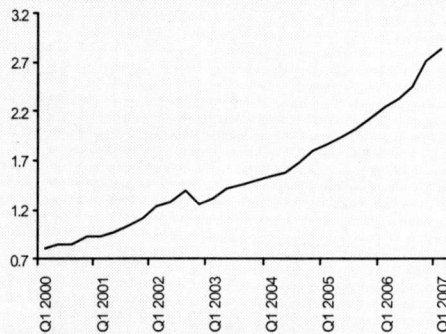

Each year households are switching about 0.4% pt of their financial assets into FX-denominated investments (Chart B). So this is a powerful structural force behind the carry trade.

A much bigger source of the yen carry trade is where Japanese banks borrow short in yen and lend long in FX (Chart C). This adds up to about $170bn annually. There are also indications that foreign banks borrow in yen to fund positions in higher-yielding currencies (worth about another $30bn). This is the big swing factor in flows out of Japan that affects the carry trade.

Chart C: Japan net crossborder banking flows, on a 12-mth sum (¥trn)

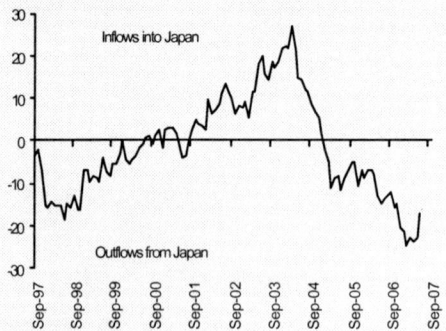

Also, contributing to the carry trade is hedging by foreign investors when buying Japanese equities or bonds (there is probably quite a lot of this as foreign net purchases of Japanese equities are strong and yet the yen is weak). As long as the yen looks weak, this hedging will continue. Overall, the yen carry trade could be around $300bn a year.

Inset 1. *Source: Datastream*

Right now, the belief in forex markets is that interest-rate differentials are the only determinant of exchange rates. The accepted wisdom is that, as long as yen interest rates and the volatility of foreign assets and their underlying currencies are low, the yen carry trade will continue.

But the correlation for the yen to the differential between Fed and BoJ policy rates is poor. There have been times when the yen has been very strong and the interest-rate differential for the US over Japan has stayed wide.

Moreover, the recent burst of yen weakness was unaccompanied by any increase in portfolio outflows. Indeed, those flows (including those of Japanese households) have actually reversed.

The reason is that much of the yen carry trade is purely speculative and not captured by Japan's payments data.

The yen carry trade is also the result of a process of creating 'synthetic yen' by offshore derivative markets. How does this work?

A mortgage borrower in a Baltic state (or Spain or Austria) can opt for a "yen" mortgage. He or she receives the credit in local currency. But the borrower pays a yen interest rate (plus a generous spread for the local bank), not the higher local currency rate. The local bank then goes into the derivatives markets and shorts the yen against an amount of its euro deposits equal to the mortgage it just granted. The bank receives the difference between local and yen rates because Japanese interest rates are lower than the local ones. Some of this interest-rate gain is passed onto the borrower and some of it the bank keeps to fatten its own margins.

The mortgage borrower assumes the asset price risk of a property, the currency risk and the interest-rate risk. The bank holds the counter-party risk on the yen trade and the risk that the borrower goes belly up. We have just witnessed the creation of synthetic yen to the value of the deposits the bank lent as "yen" mortgage.

None of this ever touched the shores of Japan or entered the Japanese BOP stats unless the counter-party to the yen trade was a Japanese bank! That means that most of the forces driving the yen down have been offshore and it happened in derivative markets.

So the best fit for forecasting the yen is now probably between the short yen positions on the Chicago Mercantile Exchange and the yen exchange rate. In other words, speculation drives the yen. That means that right now the carry trade feeds on itself.

But here is the rub. Asset bubbles some times burst of their own volition and not because of a radical shift in fundamentals such as interest rates or economic data. Such collapses usually occur after speculative fervour and volumes reach extremes driven by 'thinning' stories and after the 'insiders' have exited the trade. That is where we are on the yen carry trade right now.

Those that believe the yen carry trade will go on making them money until Japanese interest rates close the gap with the US will be proven wrong. In the ultimate stage of a bubble's life, the market itself is the only determinant of reversal, not the external data.

A bigger risk to the yen trade is that volatility of the destination currencies (like the New Zealand dollar or Hungarian forint) or assets (housing, bonds) invested in. If their volatility rises, the reward/risk ratio falls and money will exit and return to yen for safety or to repay lenders.

Once the direction of the yen changes, it will do so big time. That is not to say that there will be a repeat of the fiasco when the hedge funds were forced to reverse positions in 1998. This time, households and banks are the bigger players and are likely to reverse more gradually. Nevertheless, when the yen carry trade is over, some 13% of global liquidity will start to shrink. That will affect global asset prices, particularly in small and illiquid markets that benefited from yen inflows.

Also the damage by a rising yen will not be confined to Japanese exporters. The profit margins of small and medium businesses, which supply the blue-chip exporters and, I suspect, Japanese banks' and institutional investors' balance sheets (again!) will take a big hit.

There will be many other losers when the yen tide turns. Much other weeping will be heard in far-flung corners of the earth. The noisiest will be in the small markets and economies that are the recipients of the long side of the short yen trade: New Zealand and Indian equities and EM debt — not to mention the big losers: the dollar and US treasuries. Even the holders of yen mortgages in Spain and Austria, where they are all the rage, will feel the pain. A falling tide lowers all boats!

·

CHAPTER THREE

The Currency Accelerator

To recap our story so far: New Monetarism claims that the liquidity pyramid is shaped and sized by forces that were limited or non-existent in previous cycles. The quantity and price of money are no longer controlled by central banks. Central bank-dictated reserve ratios no longer set the credit multiplier. And hefting policy rates has not affected the cost of capital throughout the pyramid.

In the old days, liquidity was set by the reserve ratios of the central banks and the size of their power money. So total liquidity equalled power money multiplied the inverse of the reserve ratio. But now no longer!

Liquidity has no reference in the majority of its components to central bank power money. It is now a function of more abstract entities like: risk appetite, which sets leverage; currency carry trades, which set quantity; derivatives, which set risk; and market (rather than policy) interest rates, which set demand.

As long as the cost of capital remains below the natural rate of interest (which is the rate of interest at which savings equals productive rather than speculative investment), the liquidity pyramid expands more or less at the rate of demand for asset money (which can indifferently be a function of real investment demand or speculation) — Figure 20.

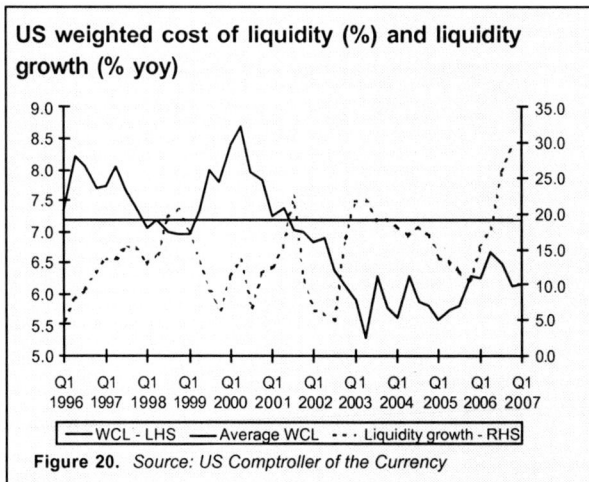

US weighted cost of liquidity (%) and liquidity growth (% yoy)

—WCL - LHS —Average WCL · · · Liquidity growth - RHS

Figure 20. *Source: US Comptroller of the Currency*

But once the cost of long-term capital rises above the natural interest rate, we should expect the liquidity pyramid to contract sharply if the expansion and contraction phrases are to be symmetrical.

If asset bubbles start to collapse, central banks, being unable to bear the economic cost (i.e. guilt), will act asymmetrically.

Central banks have been raising rates either to 'normalise' then from post 911 easy moentary policy, or to combat inflation. But at the first sign of asset price deflation, they will ease precipitously. Thus any pain of being invested in an asset bubble would be of short duration. This reinforces the markets' conviction that global monetary policy is asymmetric and biased in favour of investors and speculators.

The bond and equity bubbles

This is one reason why bond markets were (until recently) the biggest global bubble and emerging market bonds still are. By being so, bond markets prolong the credit and asset bubbles that surround us. The bond markets assume that any increase in yields (or a fall in bond prices or a rise in the long-term cost of capital) will be of short duration.

There is also another assymetric correction. The market believes that even if central bankers over-tighten monetary policy, kill the economy and create deflation, making real yields rise, it won't harm the asset (bond) price permanently (e.g. the bond holder will get his money back).

This is logical, but wrong. It's true that today corporations have little excess debt and governments will always pay up. But this ignores the impact of falling profit margins and rising cost of capital when the liquidity cycle contracts.

Indeed, yields on bonds and many other assets are now so low that the only reason to invest (and forego current consumption to do so) is if asset prices inflate further. That needs more and more liquidity to buy the existing stock of assets at ever higher prices.

THE CURRENCY ACCELERATOR

Asset prices and the cost of capital

Do asset price bubbles need the catalyst of a rising cost of capital before they burst? History shows that sometimes they do and sometimes they don't. Or more precisely, sometimes falling asset prices *coincide* with a rising cost of capital and some times they don't. So asset price bubbles can be pricked by the pin (or knife) of rising interest rates or they can be stretched so far that they burst of their own accord. Figure A shows that the Great Crash of 1929 took place in an environment of low and falling interest rates. Similarly, the Hong Kong property bust of 1993 coincided with falling interest rates (Figure B). In contrast, interest rates were on the rise when the great Nikkei bubble burst at the end of 1989 (Figure C) and when the Nasdaq burst in 2000 (Figure D).

Chart A: **US S&P-500 in the 1920s**

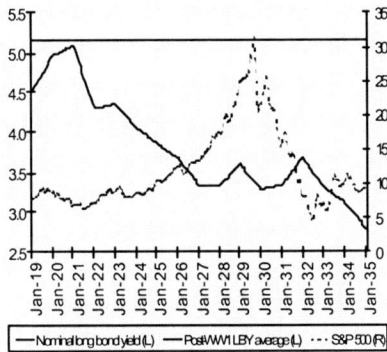

Chart B: **Hong Kong nominal 3-mth interest rate and property prices (% yoy)**

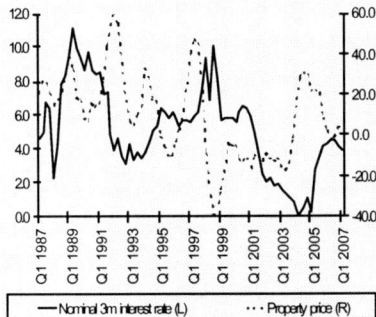

Chart C: **Japan Nikkei-225 in the 1990s**

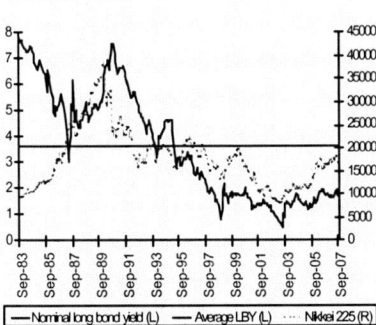

Chart D: **US Nasdaq in the 1990s**

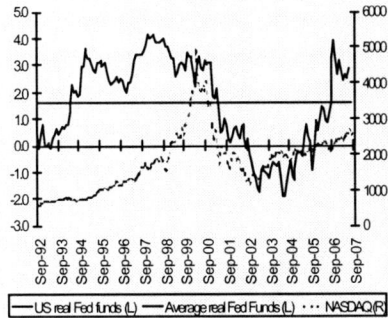

Inset 2. *Source: Robert J Shiller, Datastream, Independent Strategy*

THE CURRENCY ACCELERATOR

This is the logic of the US treasury market. As the bond market sets the pricing of much of long-term capital and is thus the fount at which all other asset bubbles drink, this logic is self-fulfilling: it is true for as long as it is true.

Of course, truth is not forever — as most divorcees who once said "I love you forever" know. Many bubbles collapse under their own weight, without rising interest rates as a catalyst (Inset 2). This one could too. A rising cost of capital is as likely to follow asset price deflation as to be the cause of it.

The currency accelerator

There's another character in our story of New Monetarism and its workings. There is a currency accelerator that modifies the traditional liquidity cycle by prolonging its expansionary phase. In so doing, it makes sure that currency turmoil will be a factor in the collapse of liquidity-driven bubbles.

Up to now, we thought that was the synapse between global liquidity and the two of the world's major sources of it — the US and Japan. But we have now discovered another link. This is the Currency Accelerator (Figure 21).

At the top of the accelerator is world GDP, split by currency. Below this is the share of each of these currency blocs in world trade. The next layer down shows in what currency each bloc pays for its imports. The amounts of each currency used to pay for the imports ends up in an exporting country.

In the current account surplus countries, it is fair to say that the foreign currency earned ends up in the central bank. Thus the final level or apex of the accelerator pyramid shows the breakdown by currency of central bank international reserves.

THE CURRENCY ACCELERATOR

As currency flows from financing GDP to international trade and then to paying for imports, it becomes increasingly concentrated in dollar and euros and to a much lesser degree in yen.

At the level of GDP, the euro and the dollar account for 46% of the value of global currency value. The US dollar and euro account for 54% of the value of international trade, but for 83% of the currencies used to pay for it. Finally, the central banks of the current account surplus world receive and keep their international reserves even more in dollars and euros (91% of the total).

In effect, the 'real' economy of global GDP and international trade cascades like water over a series of narrowing weirs that increasingly focus transaction demand for currency into two or three of the world's greatest monies. Minor currencies of countries accounting for roughly half of global output and trade are filtered out in the process. To a degree, so is

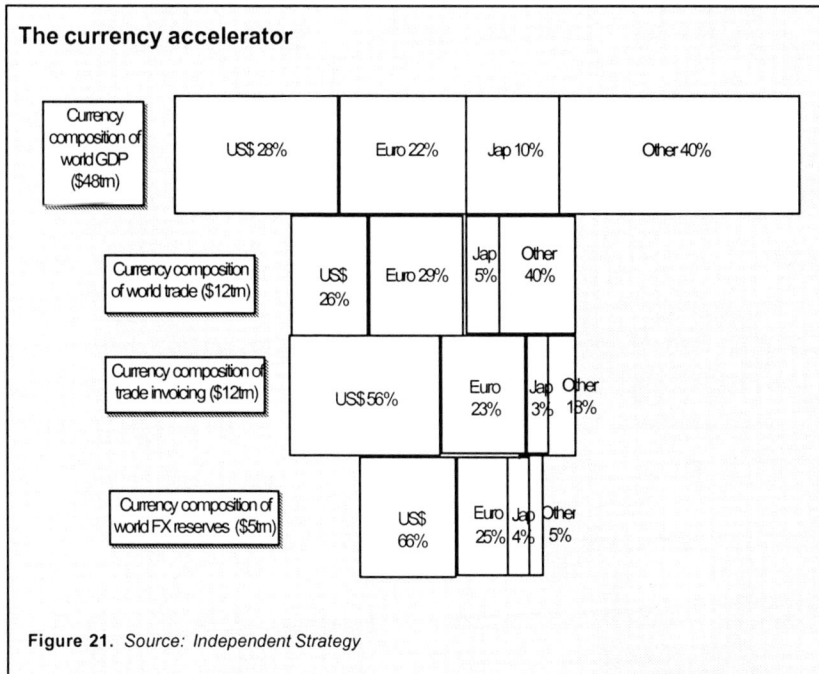

The currency accelerator

Currency composition of world GDP ($48tm)	US$ 28%	Euro 22%	Jap 10%		Other 40%
Currency composition of world trade ($12tm)	US$ 26%	Euro 29%	Jap 5%	Other 40%	
Currency composition of trade invoicing ($12tm)	US$ 56%	Euro 23%	Jap 3%	Other 18%	
Currency composition of world FX reserves ($5tm)	US$ 66%	Euro 25%	Jap 4%	Other 5%	

Figure 21. *Source: Independent Strategy*

the yen. This is a contributory reason why the yen is a naturally weak currency.

When the stream of concentrated currency reaches the portals of central banks — the point at which the water stops flowing and is stored in a reservoir — this domination of major currencies is further concentrated by central bankers in the structure of their international reserves into the three major currencies used for investment in the liquidity pyramid.

The dominant role of the euro and dollar in international trade and central bank reserves prejudices their exchange rates towards the stronger side versus the yen and other currencies. It is also ensures that the major currencies in the global liquidity pyramid enjoy remarkably low volatility.

The exchange rate of currencies is set by a combination of transaction demand for global trade and liquidity demand for asset investment. The funnelling process of international trade favours the dollar and the euro versus the yen — and it favours the stability of all three versus the world's minor currencies. This is structural for as long as it lasts.

We have seen that the currency accelerator may contribute to yen weakness by focusing transacation demand for international tarde on the dollar and the euro. the same may be temporarily true of the liquidity pyramid.

While Japanese interest rates remain very low, yen are attractive to borrow and use to fund investment in other currencies' assets that yield more. Relatively little of this yen borrowing is hedged. The yen is thus borrowed and then sold into the currency of asset being invested in. So the yen is a short. That is why it has become structurally weak despite Japan's massive current account surplus.

Currency accelerator and liquidity bust

While the mechanisms of international trade are yen negative, those of the liquidity pyramid are only so for as long as yen is the major source of finance for the carry trade.

THE CURRENCY ACCELERATOR

The 'real' economy progressively channels currency demand into the major currencies that drive global liquidity and central banks act to ensure that this pattern is preserved in the store of assets they control. Thus the global liquidity pyramid is being pumped by the mechanism of world trade.

Put it another way: liquidity is boosted by global imbalances such as the US current account deficit and Japan's massive exports of savings, both of which can be traced to underpriced capital. But for the dollar, these weak fundamentals are suppressed by "real" economy demand for dollar as a medium of transaction in international trade and as the world's predominant reserve currency. This lends the dollar some stability, which in turn means that it can be used as the major currency in the liquidity pyramid. That generates further dollar demand and, in turn, creates even more liquidity.

At the simplest level, central banks, by holding and recycling dollars (and to a lesser degree, euros and yen), are a significant part of the pyramid's stability as well as being a source of funds (Figure 23). The perception of the dollar as a stable store of wealth is the *sine qua non* of being acceptable

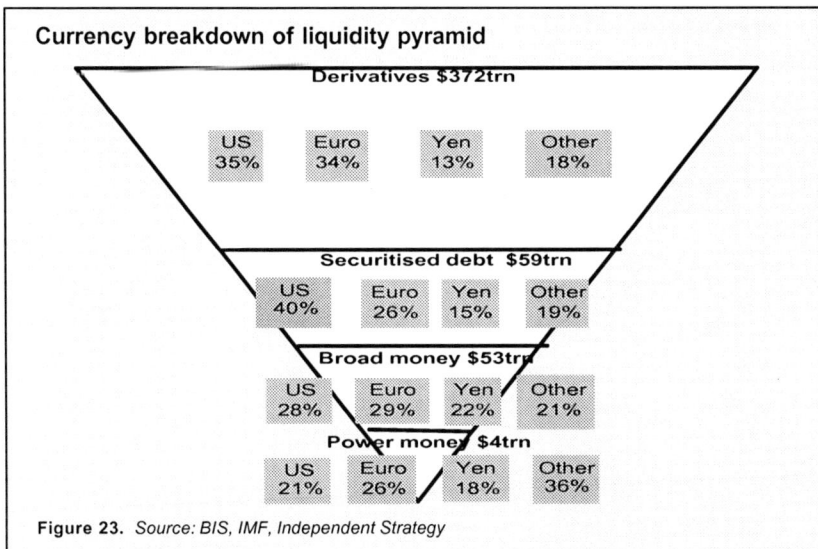

Currency breakdown of liquidity pyramid

Derivatives $372trn

| US 35% | Euro 34% | Yen 13% | Other 18% |

Securitised debt $59trn

| US 40% | Euro 26% | Yen 15% | Other 19% |

Broad money $53trn

| US 28% | Euro 29% | Yen 22% | Other 21% |

Power money $4trn

| US 21% | Euro 26% | Yen 18% | Other 36% |

Figure 23. *Source: BIS, IMF, Independent Strategy*

asset money. The liquidity pyramid would destruct overnight were central bankers to dump the dollar. This would happen despite the fact that central banks' international reserves are only a modest part of the total available liquidity in the pyramid.

As international trade expands, transaction demand grows for the currencies of the liquidity pyramid, for some more than for others. This adds to the stability of those currencies and thus increases their usability in the liquidity pyramid as asset money. This does not prevent one currency in the liquidity pyramid devaluing against another. The yen is doing so. But currencies move along a trend (weaker or stronger) with very low volatility. This means the pyramid is stable.

In another way too the liquidity function can defuse volatility from imbalances in the real economy. The over-supply of the dollar, a function of US economic imbalances, is absorbed by two demand factors: investment demand in the liquidity pyramid; and transaction demand from the real economy.

At the very least, this points to two conclusions. One is that the New Monetarism party can go on longer because 'real' economic demand for the cornucopia of currencies that form the liquidity pyramid lends stability to the whole structure. The other is that when the party ends, currency turmoil could either be a cause or an effect of the ensuing liquidity contraction, but it will for sure be a part of it, as the twin systems of trade and asset markets start to reject the weakest dominant currency — the dollar.

CHAPTER FOUR

Bubbles and the global savings glut

One of the mysteries of New Monetarism is that rising policy interest rates have had no effect on controlling the expansion of liquidity for a very long time. This was because increases in short-term rates did not cascade into the pricing of the bigger longer-term tranches in the liquidity pyramid.

In the US economy, derivatives have been used to 'freeze', at historically low interest rates, $50trn of capital or five years of GDP, as measured by the notional value of the credits represented by the interest-rate swaps. This delays the impact of Fed rate hikes. Increases in central bank interest rates remained stuck in the small, narrow apex of the pyramid occupied by central bank and short-term money. That is why liquidity continues to expand.

According to the Fed, it has removed the exceptional easing of monetary conditions that followed 9/11. Real Fed interest rates, by most measures, have returned to their long-term mean (Figure 24). But if one computes the cost of money using the interest rates that are used to price credit throughout the liquidity pyramid, particularly in its upper reaches, Fed tightening has had less of an effect.

This is hardly surprising, as the wider tranches of the pyramid do not use central

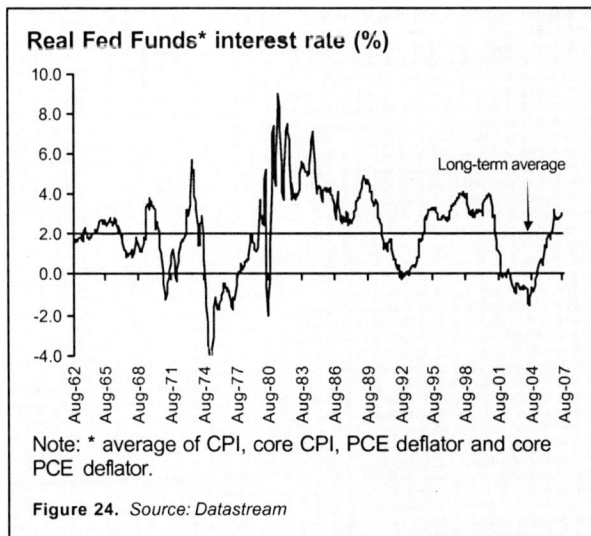

Real Fed Funds* interest rate (%)

Note: * average of CPI, core CPI, PCE deflator and core PCE deflator.

Figure 24. *Source: Datastream*

US yield curve (10-yr minus 3-mth)

Figure 25. *Source: Datastream*

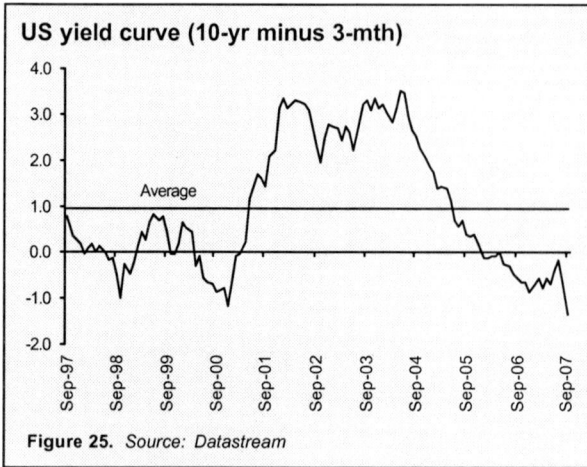

bank money. Furthermore, the growth in derivatives is overridingly in maturities beyond one year and are thus they are relatively unaffected by changes in Fed Fund rates that leave longer term rates at lower or little changed levels.

Another way of analysing the cost of money throughout the pyramid is through the yield curve. As central banks raised policy interest rates, or threatened to do so, long-term bond yields did not follow or even fell. So yield curves flattened or inverted, meaning that, as short-term money cost more, longer-term money cost the same or less (Figure 25)!

A lot of theories have been proffered on why this happened and what it means. An inverted yield curve can presage a recession. But, as the economies of US, Japan and Europe are all motoring, this seems unlikely this time.

Another explanation is the shrinking supply of long-term bonds issued by governments, together with the need for pension funds to match the maturity of assets and liabilities has increased demand for long-term securitised paper and has lowered long-term bond yields.

That may be at least part of the explanation why bond yields are so low. It explains some flatness in the yield curve, particularly in the UK. But it is too small a factor to justify it globally or even in the US. Moreover, pension funds have to match the return on assets and liabilities as much as their maturities. Today's low real rates raise doubts about pension funds' ability to achieve this when investments in long-term debt yield so little.

The global savings glut

Recently, some high-placed US officials have argued that it is a global savings glut that has kept long-term money cheap in the US, hinting that it can do so forever.

Recently, Fed Chair Ben Bernanke presented his theory of a global savings glut. It runs like this. The world is awash with surplus savings, principally in Asian emerging markets. These surplus savings flow into the US. This produces an equilibrium whereby the US has to save less and spend more to offset Asia's excessive thrift.

The existence of this Asian savings surplus has kept down US real long-term interest rates and will do so for a very long time. The US is performing a great service to the world by consuming the excess thrift of Asia which otherwise would have become a global deflationary gap *a la* Keynes.

The sub-optimal bit of this equilibrium, according to Bernanke is that the US and other ageing societies should really be saving more and so run current account surpluses and capital account deficits, as they invest in emerging markets, in order to finance their dotage. But, according to Bernanke, there is a very low risk of disruptive adjustment from this deficiency.

On the face of it, Bernanke's argument is just another version of the old shibboleth that it is the capital account surplus of the US that creates the current account deficit. It is capital flowing into the US, as the most attractive global investment destination, that obliges the US to consume so much and save so little.

That thesis can be skittled, when you consider that US financial assets no longer offer foreign investors superior returns. Indeed, foreign money

Foreign purchases of US financial assets, 1998-07 (%)

Corporate stocks 14%

Treasury bonds+notes 22%

Corporate bonds 38%

Mortgage debt 26%

Figure 26. *Source: Independent Strategy*

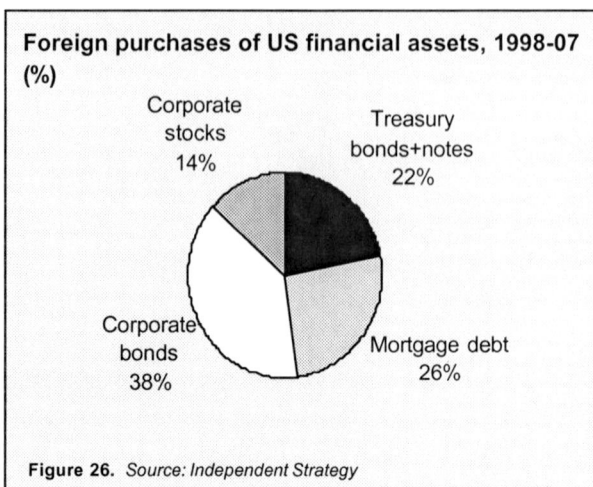

mostly flows into relatively lower-return, relatively unproductive US treasuries and mortgage instruments (Figure 26).

Anyway, surely the 20% fall in the dollar's trade-weighted index over the last three years is proof enough that the *ex post* widening of the US current account deficit is not created by an *ex ante* inflow of foreign capital. If it had, the dollar would be appreciating, not declining.

The very idea of a global savings glut has to be based on speculation (not evidence) about the *ex ante* intentions of savers and investors. *Ex post*, the world's savings and investments always balance, as witnessed by the fact that the world's current account balance nets out to zero (bar some significant statistical discrepancies).

Also Bernanke argues that it is the Asian central banks/authorities that have forced people to save more than local investment needs in the last six years. Apparently, the central banks act as intermediaries between Asian savers and the US in order to accumulate more dollar reserves as a war chest against any future crisis like they experienced in 1997.

In reality, the causal chain runs the other way: with excess US consumption creating current account surpluses in Asian economies. Then these excess dollars have to be re-invested through the hands of passive Asian central bank players (Figure 27).

BUBBLES AND THE GLOBAL SAVINGS GLUT

Let's focus upon the argument that is used to support Bernanke's key conclusion. In a nutshell, Bernanke wants to show that it is Asian surplus savings that have held down US long bond rates. Therefore the Fed is not to blame for

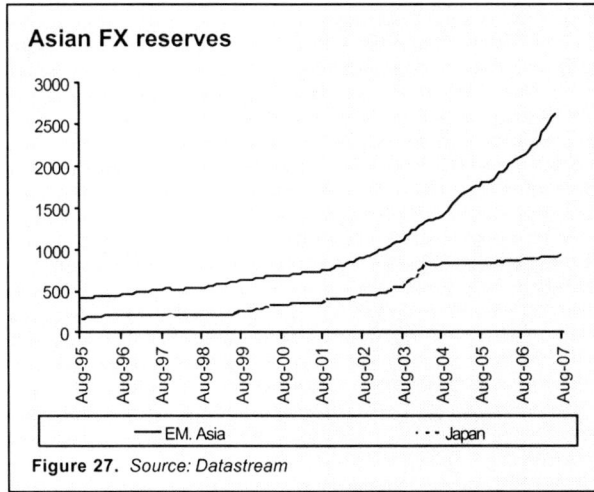

Asian FX reserves

Figure 27. *Source: Datastream*

abnormally-low interest rates. Moreover, long-term interest rates will stay low for as long as Asia's savings remain excessive, i.e. a very long time, in Bernanke's view. So there is no systemic risk from a credit bubble collapse.

But Bernanke does not justify his conclusion by any statistical analysis. Moreover, he demotes any other possible factor that could have kept real interest rates low (like lower risk premiums as inflation falls) to a footnote.

When you drop some analytical acid on the evidence, you find that the current account surpluses of Asia and OPEC (equivalent to their surplus of savings over investment) explain just 15% of the decline in US long-term real interest rates in the last 20 years. It was disinflation that did the job — disinflation and the shrinking supply of longer-dated US treasuries explained 78% of the decline (Figure 28).

Bernanke and others attribute the emergence of the global savings glut to a rise in emerging Asian economies' savings rates. Yet, in aggregate, savings rates in emerging Asia fell after 1997, despite a rise in China's and have risen only slightly since 2003 (again mainly almost completely due to China). All in all, over the whole period, they are flat.

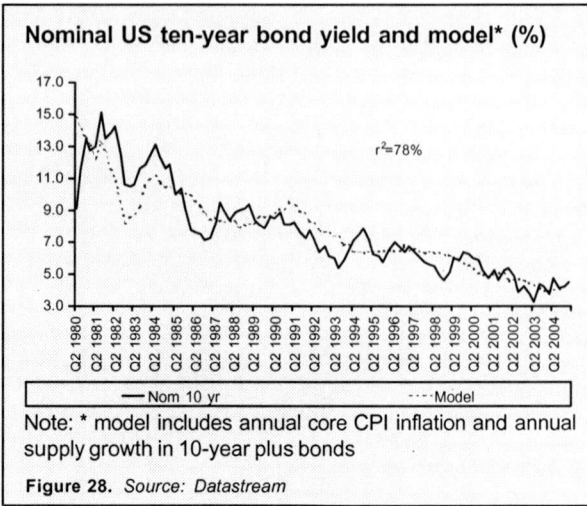

Nominal US ten-year bond yield and model* (%)

r²=78%

— Nom 10 yr   ···Model

Note: * model includes annual core CPI inflation and annual supply growth in 10-year plus bonds

Figure 28. *Source: Datastream*

In reality, like the OECD, emerging Asia had a corporate savings glut caused by falling investment, not by rising savings rates (Figure 29).

Moreover, Asia's excess corporate savings amounts to only 40% of the excess savings of the US corporate sector (Figure 30).

As emerging Asia's excess savings rates get voluntarily invested in US assets (as the liquidity pyramid says they should), they are material in keeping the dollar stable, but less important in setting US long-term interest rates. Rather than a global savings glut we should talk about a corporate dearth of investment that may be a hangover from the excess investment of the dot.com bubble and so a lot less durable than is widely appreciated.

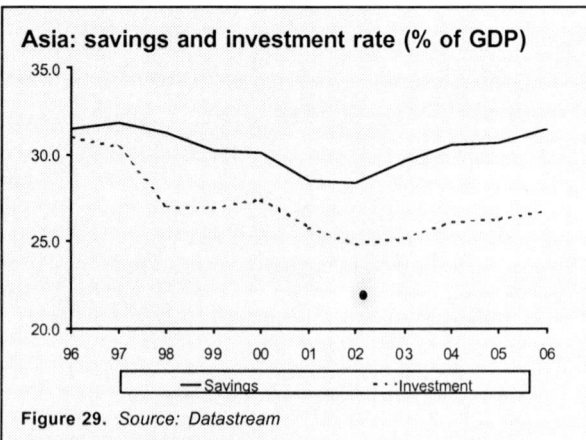

New paradigms

It is tempting to view the world's imbalances (Asia's surplus and America's dearth of savings) as the result of a new economic order whereby the rich economies

Asia: savings and investment rate (% of GDP)

— Savings   ···Investment

Figure 29. *Source: Datastream*

become shopping malls filled with old age pensioners and the emerging economies produce everything for the malls to merchandise and invest their economic gains there.

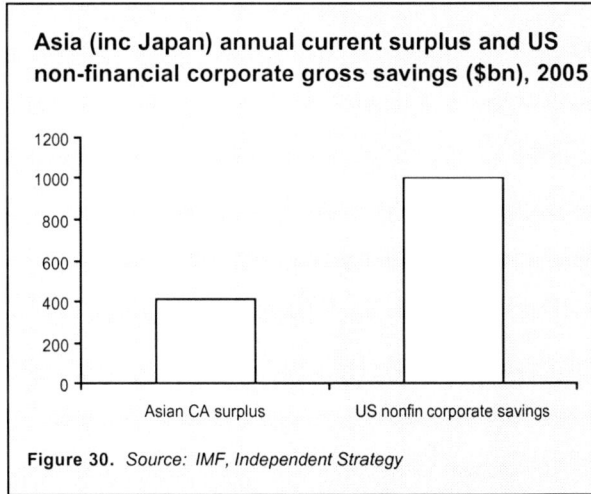

Asia (inc Japan) annual current surplus and US non-financial corporate gross savings ($bn), 2005

Figure 30. *Source: IMF, Independent Strategy*

But there is a much simpler monetary explanation that can explain all of this in terms of cash flows rather than new economic architecture. New Monetarism, by creating massive global liquidity, acts like oil in an old jalopy: it keeps it running for a while even though it's half bust.

As Japan exports cheap capital in search of higher yield, the US offers the world higher-yielding bonds than most, even if these yields are low by historical standards. Money flows to the US to keep the dollar up and US liquidity booming.

This is not a story about the economic surplus of emerging markets opting for investment in the superior productivity and returns of corporate America. It is a simple story of cash surpluses chasing higher yields (often of securities with very low capital productivity, such as a mortgage-backed security).

In 2005 and 2006, the highest yields in town were in the US. Money flowed there, keeping the dollar relatively stable by covering the US current account deficit. But this bloated the US financial system with liquidity that drove up asset prices, so keeping the US consumer borrowing and shopping.

In contrast, in China, dollars have been flowing in so fast (through export earnings and capital flows) to an economy whose GDP is less than half the size of Japan's, that the country now has more international reserves than any other country in the world.

Normally, such dollar inflows would cause the currency to rocket. But the Chinese don't want that. So the dollars are exchanged for renminbi by the central bank and then flood into domestic liquidity, while the dollars are reinvested by the monetary authorities back into the US. To do anything else, such as the central bank selling dollars into other currencies, would upset the mercantile Chinese apple cart by making its currency and exports to all dollar trade areas more expensive.

So the world economy appears to move forward seamlessly. But this is not because there is some new economic paradigm out there. Our analysis leads to diametrically opposite conclusions to those of the 'new paradigmers'. We find that the global savings glut is a product of a cyclical rise in corporate surplus savings (defined as net cash flow less investment), which will diminish when the economic cycle turns or cost inflation starts to eat into today's astronomical margins, causing profits to revert to the mean as percentage of national income.

Moreover, it was disinflation, not surplus savings, that pushed down the real cost of capital and caused asset multiples to explode over the last 20 years. And that's over too. Apart from the effect of derivatives, the main cause of low long-term interest rates is that markets are simply extraordinarily optimistic about long-term inflation (Figure 31).

Think of a ten-year US treasury bond: what is the risk of investing in it? There is no material risk of default. US government can always print money to pay its debts. The risk is that inflation will erode the value of your investment.

To compensate for this risk, long-term bond markets pay you a 'risk premium' for inflation called a 'term premium'. This is the additional

BUBBLES AND THE GLOBAL SAVINGS GLUT

yield on a long-term US treasury bond over the sum of current and future short-term (Fed) interest rates during the life of the bond.

Imagine that you thought that the Fed would always be behind the curve and would keep its interest rates below inflation. You would want long-term bond rates to be higher than present and future Fed rates to make up for this. So the bond's term premium would rise.

The same would be true if you thought that inflation would be more volatile during the life of

US ten-year bond yield (%) and term premium*

Note: * term premium = yield to maturity of long-term bond less sum of present and future Fed rates

Figure 31. *Source: Independent Strategy*

the bond. That would raise the risk that your income over the period you held the bond would be worth less in real terms or that if you were to sell at a bad time, you would get less than the par value that the US government must pay you on maturity.

Over the last decade, bond markets have become increasingly optimistic that inflation will stay low and stable. Investors have reduced the inflation risk premium on US treasuries accordingly. This is the major reason why the weighted cost of capital in the liquidity pyramid is so low. Excess corporate savings that flow into financial markets is the other.

The combination of the end of disinflation and shrinking corporate net savings will be a double blow to financial assets. The combination will lower returns and increase volatility.

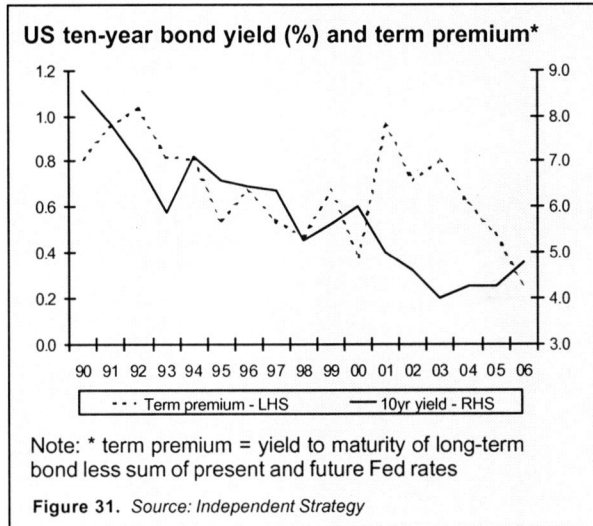

BUBBLES AND THE GLOBAL SAVINGS GLUT

CHAPTER FIVE

The magic of capitalism

Hernando de Soto in his book, *The mystery of capital*, he had one simple idea. He believed that the 'magic of capitalism' can only be unleashed by the establishment of a legal society that creates title to property. Then property can be protected, exchanged and used to raise capital efficiently.

The magic of capitalism occurs when a physical asset can at the same time become a financial asset and be turned into money (Figure 32). Thus, in De Soto's view, economic underdevelopment is closely correlated with how long it takes to transact property.

Put it this way. A Thai massage shack on a beach may be a productive asset for a family. But as long as the family can't own title to it, sell all or part of that title or borrow against it, it just remains a productive asset and not a financial one. When the Xmas 2005 *tsunami* wiped out hundreds of thousands of these poor people and their businesses, GDP in the affected countries was practically unchanged. Why? Because these 'small' people

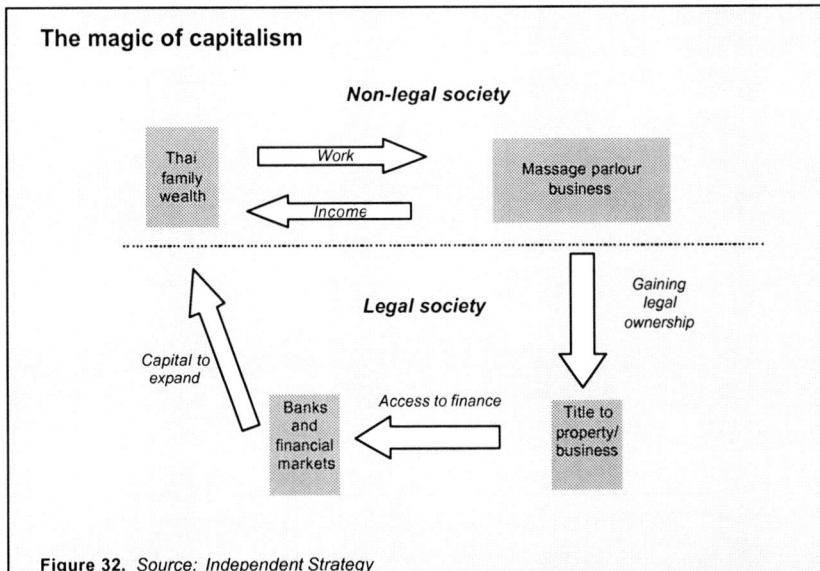

Figure 32. *Source: Independent Strategy*

and their businesses had never existed within the official economy, even though they probably constituted its backbone.

Emerging and submerging markets (and what makes them so) may provide the best proof of De Soto's law today. But a glance back through history teaches us that the US economy only took off with the codification of land ownership and the UK's with the establishment of limited partnerships. Good property law is the quintessential ingredient of good economies.

One reason communism failed (and why capitalism fails today just as abysmally) in many poor countries is that people are deprived of property, either by ideology or corruption. They are locked into their businesses but their ability to grow them, diversify their assets and advance their own well-being is curtailed. That is why micro-finance is such a brilliant concept, as it empowers the tiny asset values of small businesses.

If we may make an extension to De Soto's thinking, it is to add the concept of liquidity and particularly that of asset money. The minute that a productive asset becomes a financial asset, the concept of asset money has entered the economy: financial market liquidity has been created.

This liquidity, in turn, creates the second chapter of the value of the asset: wealth. It is only at that point that the value of the asset becomes more than a stream of income, more than just a business to earn the family's daily bread. Instead, the asset begets a second value, a capital value based on its discounted future income, which can be sold in whole or in part or borrowed against. Only then does the asset become wealth.

This kernel of De Soto's wisdom is relevant to the theory of New Monetarism and particularly to the Liquidity Pyramid. The core of New Monetarism is that much of liquidity is now destined purely towards asset investment (we call this asset money) as opposed to shopping. That is one reason why we have seen little measured inflation for the things of daily life, but rather a lot of asset price inflation in sectors like housing.

Asset money can be self-generating: its multipliers (which determine quantity), when liberated by the yield curve or driven by risk appetite, can operate independently of central banks. Asset money is also priced off medium- to long-term credit markets. So the price of asset money, and thus demand for it, is only set by central banks in so far as monetary policy influences the cost of capital for all maturities of the yield curve and in the same direction as policy rates. Recent history shows quite the opposite: central banks tighten but bond yields fall! The cost of capital in the liquidity pyramid is unaffected by central bank activity.

Black or white magic?

Today's buoyant markets for a wide range of asset classes are the result of fast liquidity expansion, particularly of asset money, which has continued even as central banks were tightening policy. The party will only stop when asset money starts to contract.

For that to happen, either the long-term cost of capital has to rise or the global economy has to tank (sapping the profit forecasts upon which asset values are currently based); or there has to be an exogenous shock to the system, reducing risk appetite and hefting the long-term cost of capital. This could be a geopolitical event (Iran, North Korea, or terrorism) but durable in its economic fallout (e.g. a sustained rise in the cost of energy). There could also be a spontaneous collapse in asset bubbles.

Also, liquidity contraction could stem from the collapse of the leverage loan market through regulatory change or because a few overgeared mega-deals go sour.

However, if none of these things were to happen and central banks stopped tightening for good reason, a new expansionary liquidity cycle could begin without contraction of the old one. Many would view this as simply the continuation of the process of unlocking value from a long list of assets that have not yet been touched by the De Soto magic. Others would see in it the prolonging of asset bubbles that will be bigger and more dangerous for the global economy when they finally deflate. Which is it?

The 'liquidity pyramid' merely symbolises a mechanical arrangement, albeit complex, of financial intermediaries and markets — exactly those that add the ingredient of magic to De Soto's capitalism. But when does it add too much liquidity? When does the white magic become black?

The answer to this question is neither clear nor universal. How universal are recent asset bubbles? A fair number of global bubbles have already burst, among them housing in Australia, the UK and the US and parts of Europe, as well as the dot.com equity bubble of the late 1990s and industrial raw materials, such as copper. Yet the global financial system and economy appear to be in rude health.

If we use derivative and securitised debt markets as a proxy for all asset money, then the vast majority of such liquidity is being created in Europe and the US.

Few of the tools of New Monetarism took hold in Asia. As a result, many assets (among them housing) failed to join the global liquidity party. This was partly due to the existence of asset price deflation in Japan for much of the decade and in non-Japan Asia after the 1997 Asian crisis. Paucity of asset money creation was also due to Asia's less-developed financial institutional framework.

The benefits of De Soto's magic will permeate the Asian region in the next great liquidity cycle with the advent of markets for securitised mortgages and derivatives and rising leveraged buyout activity.

Japan has one of the most undeveloped, least leveraged, housing markets in the developed world. This is totally out of step with the ongoing convergence of global youth towards common culture and living norms.

Ex-communist Europe is another area with high rates of home ownership and low levels of mortgage debt. This housing market will also become liquefied in the next cycle to the benefit of lenders and consumers and to the detriment of the region's current account deficits.

But there the good news ends. We may not have a universal asset bubble, but we do have universal liquidity! Despite the focus of new asset money in the EU and US, the absolute amount of liquidity, which we estimate at around ten years of global GDP, means that it will hurt all regions once it contracts. The riskier and less-developed financial markets and economies will suffer most. The God of economics lays no claim to being just.

Defining and measuring bubbles

How do we judge if the cornucopia of asset money we describe is an inherent source of future financial instability of a magnitude that would seriously hurt the global economy?

According to seminal research at the Bank of International Settlements, when credit growth is significantly above trend, it is a very good indicator of financial or economic crises to come (see Inset 3 on page 52). BIS researchers found that when credit growth is 4-5 percentage points above trend or asset prices are 40-50% above trend, it predicted nearly 80% of crises within a time horizon of one to three years (Inset 3, Figure A). Although BIS researchers used a more traditional definition of liquidity than we do (basing their study on money aggregates), it still makes sense that too much money chasing too few assets is the *Ursprung* of all financial crises.

Applying this model today indicates that we are into dangerous waters in the US (Inset 3, Figure B). Modifying the definition of credit to include securitised debt and derivatives reinforces that message (Inset 3, Figure C).

THE MAGIC OF CAPITALISM

Bubbles and crises

BIS researchers, Borio and Lowe, looked at the long-term relationship between credit growth in the G10 economies and the movement of asset prices. They found that there were 38 crisis episodes between 1970 and 1999 spread over 27 countries. They found that when credit as a % of GDP grew to 4-5% points above trend, it was followed by some form of financial crisis on nearly 80% of occasions within one year. When several factors are combined (credit, asset prices and the exchange-rate), the probability of a crisis (either banking or economic) was still around 40% two years out and around 70% four years out (Figure A).

Figure A: **Probability of crisis in industrial countries for 2,3,4 years after (%)**

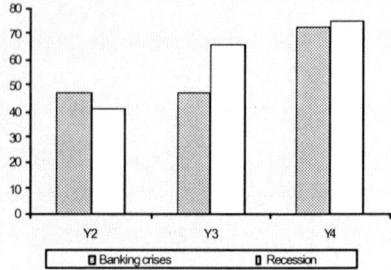

We looked at long-term credit data for the US. That did show the deviation from trend has never been higher than now (Figure B). And when measuring the total liquidity pyramid (including derivatives), the deviation from trend is also near record levels (Figure C).

Figure B: **US domestic private credit/GDP (% deviation from trend)**

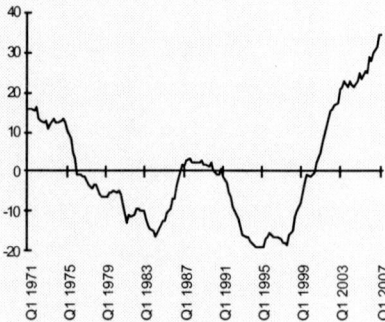

Figure C: **Total US liquidity/ GDP and net household worth/ GDP deviation from trend (%)**

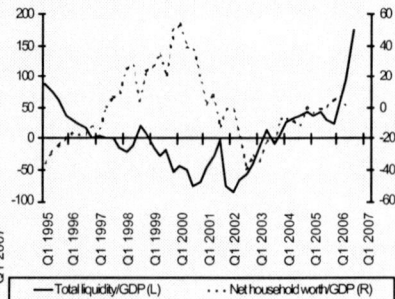

Inset 3. *Source: Datastream, BIS*

But if excess credit is the cause of financial crisis, then it must first manifest itself in asset bubbles — right? Defining a bubble is a good place to answer that.

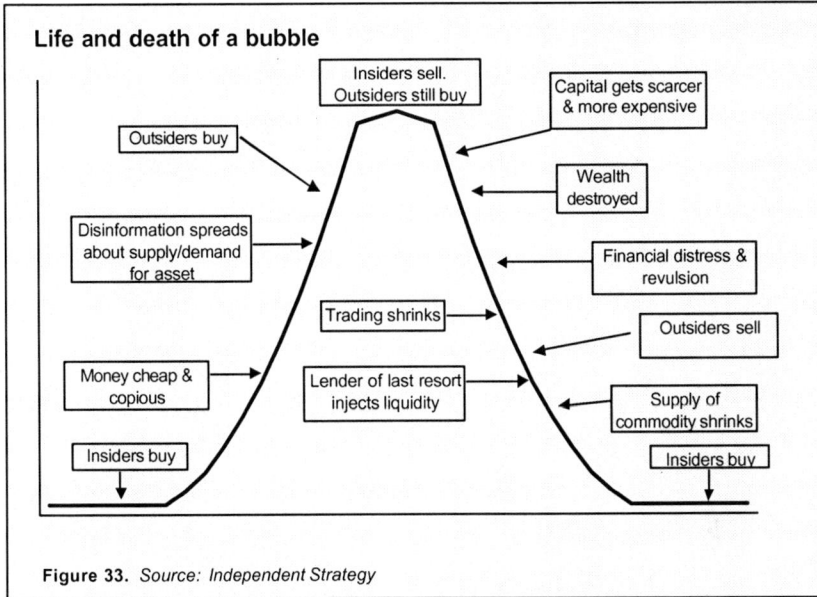

Figure 33. *Source: Independent Strategy*

Charles Kindleberger is recognised as 'Mr Bubble' among economists. The Kindleberger definition of a bubble is "a sharp rise in price of an asset or a range of assets in a continuous process, with the initial rise generating expectations of further rises and attracting new buyers — generally speculators interested in profits from trading in the asset rather than its use or earning capacity".

The life of a bubble can also be charted (Figure 33). If the BIS model is right, we should be somewhere near the peak with abnormal high returns on a variety of assets and high turnover based on increasingly flimsy stories.

Double-bubbles and reefs

To trawl the great financial seas for asset bubbles, we should look for assets where 1) valuations are much higher than fundamentals warrant; 2) trading volumes are abnormally high; and 3) returns are off the map. We did this and came up with no significant bubbles currently in equities or bonds and only a few in housing, commodity and energy markets.

THE MAGIC OF CAPITALISM

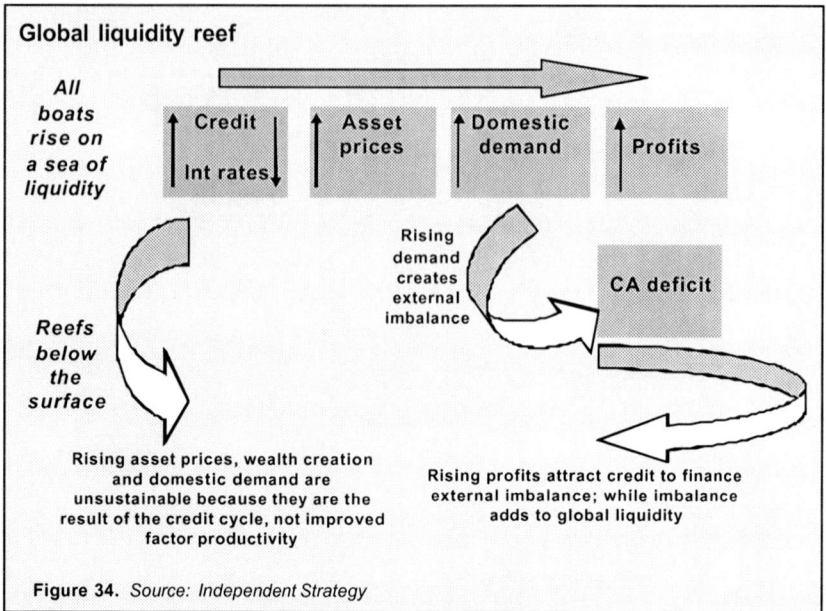

Global liquidity reef

All boats rise on a sea of liquidity

| ↑ Credit | ↑ Asset | ↑ Domestic | |
| Int rates↓ | prices | demand | ↑ Profits |

Rising demand creates external imbalance

CA deficit

Reefs below the surface

Rising asset prices, wealth creation and domestic demand are unsustainable because they are the result of the credit cycle, not improved factor productivity

Rising profits attract credit to finance external imbalance; while imbalance adds to global liquidity

Figure 34. *Source: Independent Strategy*

How come there are few bubbles if both traditionally-defined credit in the US and the liquidity pyramid globally are expanding at double-digit percentage rates (well above trend) and the cost of capital is still well below the natural rate?

The answer lies in the existence of reefs as opposed to bubbles. Reefs are financial disequilibria that are hidden from view due to the high level of liquidity, but have serious consequences for the real economy when liquidity ebbs (Figure 34). The characteristic of a reef is that, to the extent that excess liquidity permeates all the drivers of the economy, the less bubbles will appear and the greater will be the economic damage that will be inflicted by a reversal of the 'credit' cycle.

Its lesson is clear: if the tide of liquidity lifts all economic boats proportionately, then their individual relative valuations to each other will not appear unreasonable. All that is needed to maintain an aura of reason is for the 'credit cycle' to boost asset prices, wealth, economic activity, income and profit at the same time and proportionately (i.e.

preserving traditional valuation cross-relationships). If this happens, valuations will not signal the existence of bubbles. Instead of being reassuring, this indicates that the dangers are more widespread, affecting a greater number of economic variables.

If the increase in asset values were the result of factor productivity gains rather than liquidity, the boost to the economy would be rock solid. But if it were down to liquidity, then, although relative valuations may not signal bubbles, it is likely that economic imbalances like a current account deficit will.

History offers some evidence that this theory of reefs works in reality. IMF research indicates that only one-third of a wide range of stock market crashes since 1800 were associated with a previous bubble. Yet 50% of equity crashes were associated with recessions.

Today, we are at the end of the twin decades of disinflation. Throughout this period, asset values were justifiably boosted by falling inflation and the cost of capital and rising capitalisation rates that reflected increases in the present values of income streams. Productivity increased in tandem.

But in recent years, particularly since 911, liquidity has taken over as the engine of asset prices. This makes any judgement of how much of asset values is real (and sustainable) or just the result of excess liqudity (and unsustainable) difficult to make.

All bubbles (and reefs) are financed by copious credit. In Kindleberger's words, the process (of creating new forms of money and credit) is endless: "fix any 'M' and the market will create new forms of money in periods of boom to get around the limit and create the necessity to fix a new variable M1". In the words of the 19th century commentator, Walter Bagehot, "men of business in England do not like the currency question. They are perplexed to define accurately what money is: how to count they know, but what to count they do not know".

THE MAGIC OF CAPITALISM

In order for bubbles and reefs to develop, credit must be plentiful. But it need not be cheap (in either real or nominal terms) judged by historical standards. Investors need only be convinced that credit is cheap relative to forecast gains on the assets they invest in.

In other words, credit need only be cheap when deflated by anticipated asset price inflation. Asset price inflation may be totally divorced from consumer prices throughout the bubble period, the former being high and the latter often being low. A case in point was the Japanese bubble economy of the 1980s.

Today, most long-term bond yields are low by historical standards. Yet bond market returns to investors are way below the levels that normally characterise a bubble. This is typical of a reef valuation — excessively priced by historical standards, but stable and with little evidence of 'mania'.

Consequently, successful pursuit of stable and low consumer price inflation by central banks is not synonymous with eschewing asset price bubbles or achieving financial stability. Bubbles and reefs thrive in the calm waters of low or falling inflation.

Low and stable inflation can engender excessive liquidity because it boosts confidence to borrow and lend. It can also enhance confidence in economic prospects and lead to supply-side improvements, both of which may attract foreign capital and add to asset price pressure.

Low inflation can also boost confidence in the conduct of monetary policy and make investors over-confident that interest rates will remain low forever. Indeed, many of the world's worst bubbles developed under such conditions.

The Japanese bubble economy grew like Topsy, while CPI inflation fell or stayed low (interest rates were relatively high, but falling). The Nikkei took off in early 1986 as the CPI index moved into negative territory.

The stock market only cracked when inflation moved up towards 4% in 1989. Nominal bond yields were still near decade lows when the Nikkei burst.

Liquidity and valuations

What does the cheapness of credit do to asset valuations? Take two US examples: equities and housing. If equities are valued using current long-term interest rates to discount profits, they appear undervalued. However, if the exercise is redone using a 'normalised' (20-year long-term average) bond yield, equities appear overvalued.

The same goes for housing. If affordability is calculated using mortgage rates, a house can look cheap. But if the price of the same house is compared to income, it can look expensive.

That is why at the peak of the US housing bubble the bullish 'fundamentalists' were declaring US housing not to be a bubble (finding the usual 'fundamentals' to justify their views — like Latino immigration). The bears, on the other hand, comparing house prices to income, claimed housing was overpriced for equally fundamental reasons.

In reality, the bulls were seeking to justify overpriced housing by reference to underpriced capital. Thus one bubble made another's valuation look reasonable. This is the 'double-bubble valuation jeopardy'.

The analysis can be broadened to include other assets. If asset markets rise because people have confidence in fundamentals, the result will be the creation of wealth and more confidence. This will be borrowed against (or assets will be liquidated or equity withdrawn) and spent, thus boosting economic activity and profits. Thus rising asset prices lift all relative prices, profits and activity proportionately, thus hiding bubbles under the reef (Figure 35).

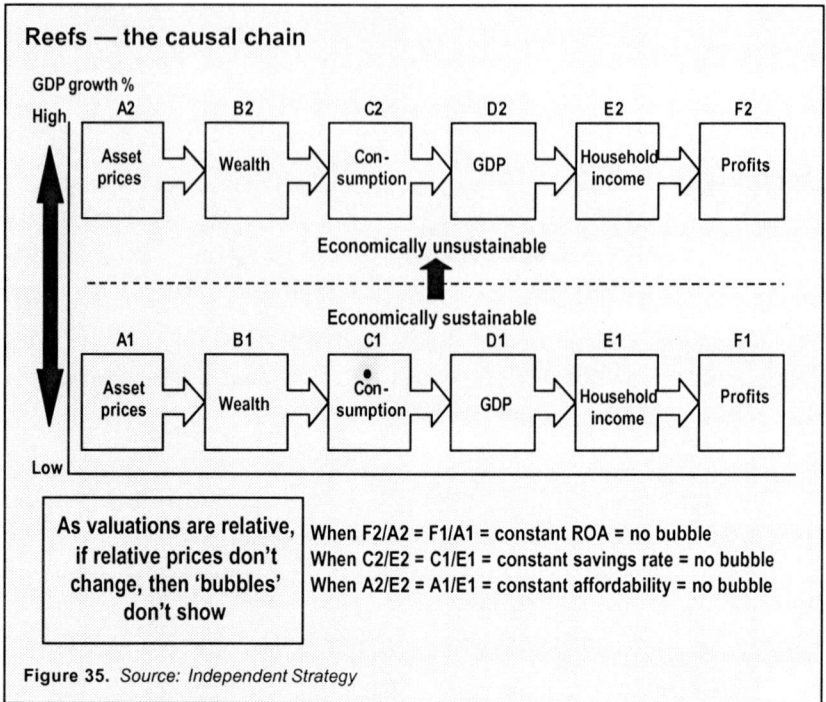

Reefs — the causal chain

GDP growth %

A2	B2	C2	D2	E2	F2
Asset prices	Wealth	Con-sumption	GDP	Household income	Profits

Economically unsustainable

- -

Economically sustainable

A1	B1	C1	D1	E1	F1
Asset prices	Wealth	Con-sumption	GDP	Household income	Profits

As valuations are relative, if relative prices don't change, then 'bubbles' don't show

When F2/A2 = F1/A1 = constant ROA = no bubble
When C2/E2 = C1/E1 = constant savings rate = no bubble
When A2/E2 = A1/E1 = constant affordability = no bubble

Figure 35. *Source: Independent Strategy*

So are equities cheap or expensive now? The answer is a yawn more often than not because valuation is such a doubtful indicator of where the market is headed and an even worse predictor of crises. But right now, it is interesting.

Global P/Es have more or less reverted to the mean after the equity bubble crash of 2000 and the following years of solid earnings growth. So the P/E valuation looks reasonable. But the last ten years of equity prices include a very large slice of bubble years in which valuations were absurdly high. Therefore, in order to be cheap, P/Es today should lie well below the last decade's mean average.

The same applies to profits. Today's profits are peak of cycle — unless you believe the cycle is dead. Cut them by 20-40% (a typical cyclical reversal) and equities don't look so cheap any more (Figure 36).

Most important of all, the last decade was a time of disinflation. Disinflation boosts prices for assets by a multiple of the income they generate, because it increases the present value of future earnings dramatically. Therefore, there is a strong upward bias in the historical data for P/Es that will not be repeated in the post-disinflationary world.

US P/E multiple

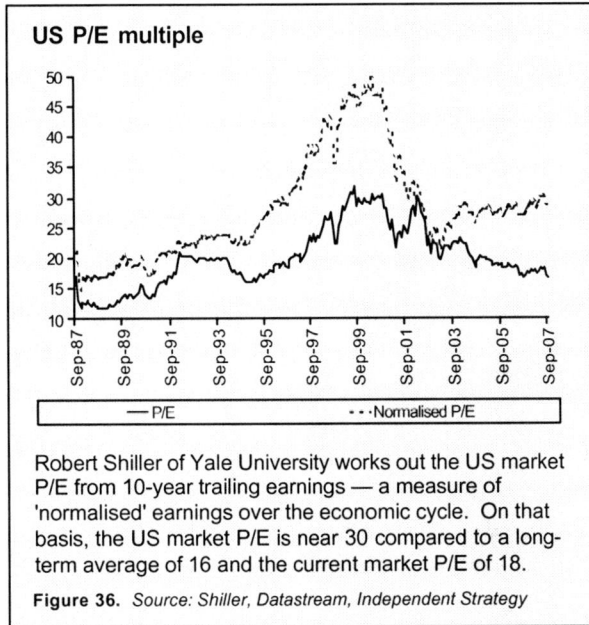

Robert Shiller of Yale University works out the US market P/E from 10-year trailing earnings — a measure of 'normalised' earnings over the economic cycle. On that basis, the US market P/E is near 30 compared to a long-term average of 16 and the current market P/E of 18.

Figure 36. *Source: Shiller, Datastream, Independent Strategy*

There are some who find equities are cheap because all manner of equity yields (dividend, earnings, cash flow) are deep in undervalued territory once they are adjusted by real or nominal interest rates — long or short. If P/E ratios are turned upside down into earnings yields and then related to long-term bond yields, then equities look super cheap.

Today's government bond markets offer rates of return well below the long-term average natural rate of interest. Poorer-quality bond markets add greatly to this disequilibrium by underpricing risk and offering very low yield spreads on non-sovereign issues over treasuries. This means that, with the exception of policy rates set by the Fed, credit is very cheap by historical standards and in abundant supply across all market segments and all along the yield curve.

The trouble with this analysis is that it seeks to justify post-bubble equities as being underpriced by reference to a massive bubble in the bond market.

Is it rational that the foreign debt of some of the most unviable states in the world is selling at spreads that are at all-time lows to US treasuries? Is today's fixed income market really is a good benchmark for judging equities?

So much for the standard stable of equity valuation measures. They tell us very little right now about where equity markets are going or what they are worth. "Garbage in means garbage out" to use a cliché.

Cost of equity

A more interesting avenue to explore is the widening dichotomy between corporate return on equity and the cost of equity.

It is a truism of capitalism that a corporation is just covering its cost of capital when the market value of its assets equals the cost of replacing them. When that happens, the return on company equity invested equals the cost of buying that equity. In contrast, the historic value of assets, as they are recorded in the balance sheets, rarely represents either the market value or the replacement cost accurately. Nevertheless, it does provide a benchmark for judging deviations.

Yet in all major markets (and we present the data for the three biggest), the corporate return on equity (ROE) has trended up and now exceeds the cost of equity (COE) by a wide margin (Figure 37).

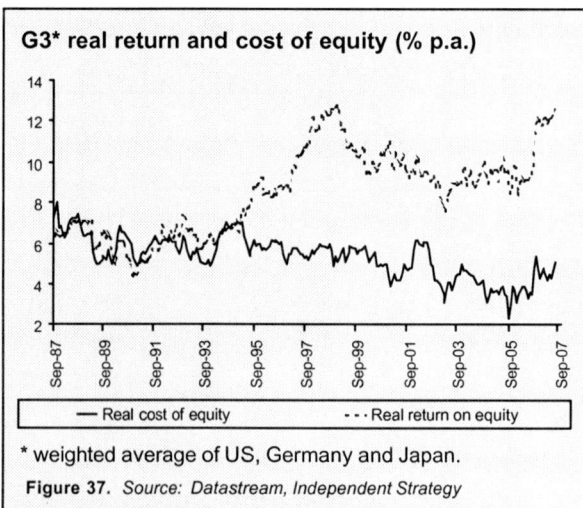

G3* real return and cost of equity (% p.a.)

— Real cost of equity   · · · Real return on equity

* weighted average of US, Germany and Japan.

Figure 37. *Source: Datastream, Independent Strategy*

What caused this to happen? The first possibility is wonky data, making this series as unreliable as all the others. How could the data be wrong? Corporate return on equity is a matter of historical record. It merits the caveat attached to any macro series based on traditional accounting methodology. But the trend is probably reliable.

The cost of equity is another matter. It is always a wild guess. In order to estimate it for each market, we can use the risk-free, long-term government bond yield plus the historical equity risk premium. Could this be inaccurate? Government bond yields are "known". So the "unknown" in COE is the equity risk premium. To close the gap between COE and ROE, the equity risk premium would have to increase pretty dramatically to push the COE close to ROE. That seems unlikely, as volatility has been falling for equities, even in relation to bonds, which is what the equity risk premium compensates for.

What would it mean if corporate ROE is really so much greater than COE? Corporations are creating an added value for their owners, much like an economic rent, by making more money than it costs them to make it. Great while it lasts, but this should inspire profit-maximising management to go on an investment binge until the marginal return of the last unit of investment equals the marginal cost of capital used to make it.

This thinking underpins, as often as not subliminally, the wedge of opinion that supposes global business investment will take over the running in the world economy, so replacing the US consumer. And yet the 'corporate investment binge' has not happened. The divergence of ROE and COE is now nearly two decades old in the US (where investment to GDP has since done nothing) and a decade old in Europe and Japan.

Back in the 1970s, the market value of equity was a fraction of the replacement value of equity and even at times ran below the historical COE recorded in the books. The reason was simple: inflation was eroding the real earnings of corporations so that they could not cover the replacement cost of the assets needed to do their business. Then along came disinflation and the market value of equity rose above both the replacement value and the historical cost of equity.

Disinflation allowed corporations to earn real returns on their assets. It did so by reducing the relative cost of those assets (the cost of capital equipment fell in relation to most output costs while technological progress improved its performance). Disinflation also helped generate productivity gains that reduced other costs (such as labour) of doing business. So unit costs were reduced by more than their output prices. Consequently, the profit share in national income rose at the expense of labour's share.

But there was something else at work here. As mentioned above, disinflation boosted asset values in relation to income dramatically. This happened because both inflation and real interest rates fell for two decades. This increased the present value of future income and made assets worth more.

Even if the asset was a house, which earns a rental income and enjoys little or no productivity gains, its value rose in relation to the earnings stream it generated (or could potentially generate) thanks to disinflation.

When capital became seriously underpriced at the end of the disinflationary period, so did the discount factor for future earnings. We then entered a period of asset price inflation.

Today, it appears that the market recognises asset price inflation as a gain, but not as business cost. That is why equity market prices today are still so much in excess of book value. Were the market to consider asset price increases as a cost, rather than just a hidden profit, it would adjust depreciation charges up and profits down.

This is rather like broader society. Many recognise that asset price inflation is fairly widespread, but few believe that this is a cost to society. This is hardly surprising, as many of us own the assets and benefit from the wealth increases that asset price inflation creates. Indeed, we have derived measures of inflation, such as the housing component of US CPI, that all but exclude asset price inflation.

Thus, we have conditioned ourselves (and our central bankers) to believe in the non-inflationary consequence of asset price inflation. But the grim reaper of reality never rides behind the fair maiden of illusion for long. If the prices of the assets used to produce are inflating, so ultimately must costs.

Volatility

It is time to bring volatility into the equation. In the last four years the volatility of financial markets has fallen dramatically and to levels not seen since the mid-1990s (Figure 38). Derivative spreads, particularly for those that offer insurance against changes in interest rates (e.g. swaps) and against default (CDSs), collapsed. Currency volatility for developed and undeveloped economies dropped too.

Low volatility increases the self-generating capacity of the liquidity pyramid. Take just three examples. Low volatility may decrease the cost of buying insurance in derivative markets. If it costs less to do so, the financial sector will buy more insurance (against default and rising rates). By removing most of these risks (collateral risk remains) from the balance sheet, financial intermediaries can create new credit because their stock of risk assets to their equity and reserves is held down relative to their rising loan book.

On a wider scale, the low cost of locking in a stable

Volatility			
Equity markets since 1959	US	Jap	Ger
Mean volatility (% pts)	13.19	14.13	16.78
Current volatility	10.07	13.66	12.77
Bond markets since 1986	US	Jap	Ger
Mean volatility (% pts)	4.48	3.14	3.26
Current volatility	3.88	1.94	2.94
Currency markets since 1971 (% vs dollar)	Jap	Ger	UK
Mean volatility	9.39	9.70	8.61
Current volatility	9.20	8.81	8.27

Figure 38. Source: IMF

cost of financing, using instruments such as interest-rate swaps, will encourage more players to inoculate their business against a future rise in rates. Again, this facilitates higher levels of leverage, not only in corporations, but also in the leveraged buyout and private equity sectors.

Finally, much of the creation of liquidity in the pyramid relies upon borrowing in one asset — normally a low-yielding one — and investing in another higher-yielding one. A Japanese bank investing yen deposits in US treasuries is doing just that. Doing so adds to US liquidity without currently diminishing Japan's because bank deposits in Japan were fallow money that no one wanted to borrow. So lending it to Uncle Sam did not change Japan's liquidity.

But if anything raises volatility durably, the impact on liquidity would be severe because of the engineering of the liquidity pyramid. This impact would be quite independent of the cause of increased volatility.

To assess the risk of higher volatility we should first look at why it has fallen in recent years. First, greater macro economic stability (often referred to as the Great Moderation) — the volatility of economies (growth, inflation, interest rates etc) fell by as much as financial market volatility (but earlier).

Second, more targeted and more transparent monetary policy management also made for less market shocks. Third, there was more stable corporate performance and improved profitability, due to productivity gains from better resource utilisation, lower leverage, better inventory management etc.

And finally, there were financial factors. Improved liquidity and risk dispersion due to new market participants (e.g. hedge funds specialising in insurance products) and new products (e.g. derivatives such as CDOs, CDSs etc) allowed market participants to unbundle, hedge and disperse risk throughout the financial system (the US mortgage backed security (MBS) and derivatives based on them being the single largest example).

THE MAGIC OF CAPITALISM

Recent research downplays the impact of the macroeconomic Great Moderation because it happened much earlier than the corresponding fall in volatility in financial markets. On the other hand, the idea that financial factors are at least partially responsible for low financial market volatility means that it is the architecture of the liquidity pyramid itself that creates the low volatility, upon which it depends for much of its ability to generate liquidity (Figure 39)!

Before pooh poohing the idea, it is as well to remember that in the course of the last five years the financial system has weathered umpteen macro and micro shocks with hardly a tremor. So far, the regulators' contention has proven correct that derivatives diminish systemic risk in the financial system by removing concentrated risk from banks and spreading it among multiple players better equipped to handle it.

Our own view, to echo Hyman Minsky, is that there is nothing more likely to produce instability than a lengthy period of stability. Much of the pricing of credit in today's markets seems grossly out of kilter with risk

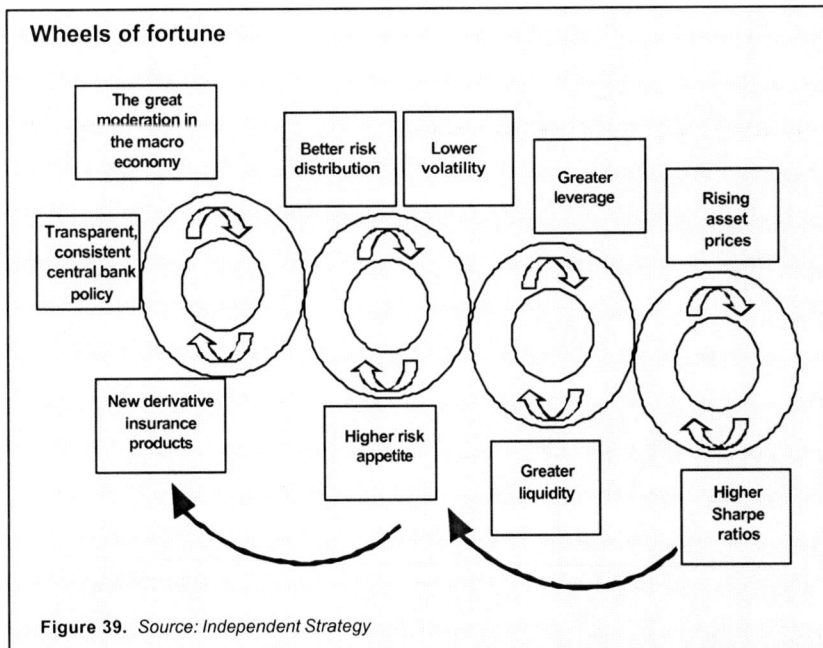

Figure 39. *Source: Independent Strategy*

— and that includes credit derivatives and much of the financing of leverage buyouts and private equity deals as well as emerging market bonds.

What the entire system (symbolised in the liquidity pyramid) has not been stress-tested for is a generalised rise in the cost of capital. Many private equity deals being done today can be proven on the back of an envelope to be unprofitable if long-term cost of capital and risk spreads return to the mean. And we view this as a question of 'when' and not 'if'.

CHAPTER SIX

Reversing the liquidity cycle

The main theme of this booklet is that the new forms of money or liquidity that have come to dominate the macroeconomic and financial world are not here to stay. They are a product of serendipity or a fortuous combination of events — namely, disinflation since the early 1980s, US political hegemony since the 1990s after the collapse of the commmunist regimes; the economic rise of China since 1992; and the dissaving of America's households since the millennium.

None of these phenomena is here for eternity or even for more than a few decades. And in the case of disinflation, US political dominance and American household spending, their days are already over. That's why we are not in any 'new paradigm'. The bubbles of New Monetarism will eventually burst (some have already: US housing). And the flows of liquidity will eventually break the banks of the weirs they are held in and then dry up.

The events that could cause liquidity to contract are close encounters of a daily kind. As we have discussed, many bubbles burst of their own volition. And most financial crises that result in recession or depression were not preceded by easily identifiable bubbles, just an excessive credit cycle. The burst happens simply: one day people come to market and the pigs are too dear. So they stop buying pigs.

A higher long-term cost of capital

A generalised rise in the cost of capital would also do the trick. Derivative pricing is highly dependent on two to five-year money staying cheap.

The key driver of a rise in the cost of capital would be inflation. Higher inflation could be the result of the US economy being stronger than the market anticipates, Europe powering ahead and Japan catching up. That would close the global resource gap smartly (Figure 40) and could start to generate inflation (as measured by the traditional yardstick).

Rising inflation could also be the result of the dissipation of the world's cheap goods markets. Globalisation and China have been the mantra for the view that prices of goods in world markets will continue to fall and stay low. However, this sanguine view of Chinese export prices may well be overdone.

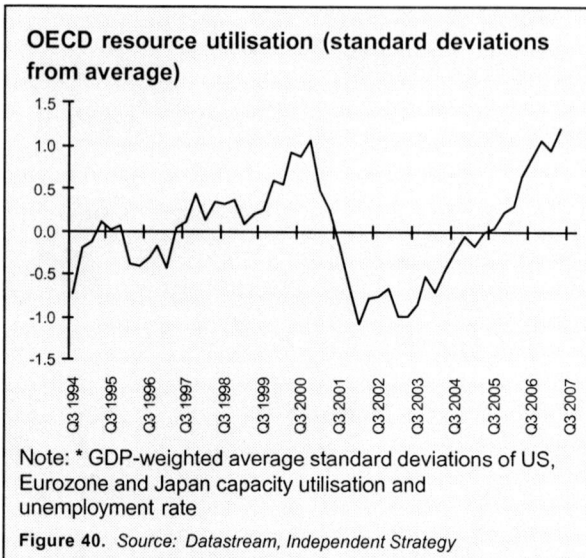

OECD resource utilisation (standard deviations from average)

Note: * GDP-weighted average standard deviations of US, Eurozone and Japan capacity utilisation and unemployment rate

Figure 40. *Source: Datastream, Independent Strategy*

China's export prices are rising (Figure 41). That will eventually have an effect on OECD inflation. If inflationary expectations (which have remained low) start to move higher, risk premiums on long-term capital will rise and that will hit financial markets hard, especially given the excessive expansion in liquidity.

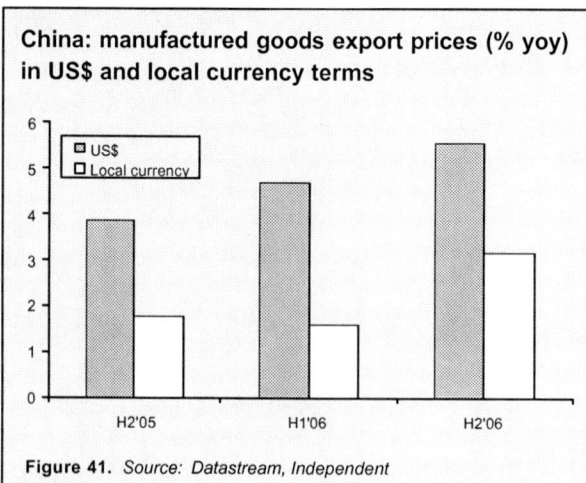

China: manufactured goods export prices (% yoy) in US$ and local currency terms

Figure 41. *Source: Datastream, Independent*

On China's eastern seaboard production costs are soaring. That suggests that China's huge potential additions to the global labour force are not destined to push down tradable goods prices forever.

This does not mean that a pair of jeans made in China won't remain relatively cheap, but rather that they will be getting more expensive (and that's the measure of inflation) .

This would have a significant impact on the pricing of goods globally because most other areas of the world (particularly the US) are experiencing rising unit labour costs and need to increase output prices (i.e. inducing inflation) to maintain their margins. Already US corporate output prices have started to rise much faster than measured consumer inflation. A shift from deflation to inflation by competing goods from China would return pricing power to competing corporations in developed countries to some degree.

This scenario, always a slow-burn one, seems to be gradually unfolding. China's domestic manufacturing PPI, total PPI and RPI all seem to have bottomed around January 2006 and to have been rising since. This has happened before with little or no impact on export prices.

But this time it is different. China's export prices since 2005 have been rising by 2.5-3.0% in renminbi terms. The renminbi has also been strengthening. So, in US dollar terms, China's export prices are increasing by more than 5%.

Just to make sure this was not due to some mismeasurement unique to China's Statistics Bureau, such as failure to allow for the impact of China's exports shifting from low to high value-added goods, we tested export prices for other Asian countries. The story is the same and looks very much a carbon copy of what is happening in China (Figure 42).

There are good reasons for this. The labour productivity cycle peaked in most of Asia in late 2005 and early 2006 and nearly all non-Japanese Asian unit labour costs are now rising.

REVERSING THE LIQUIDITY CYCLE

Emerging Asia (ex China): manufactured goods export prices (% yoy) in US$ and local currency terms

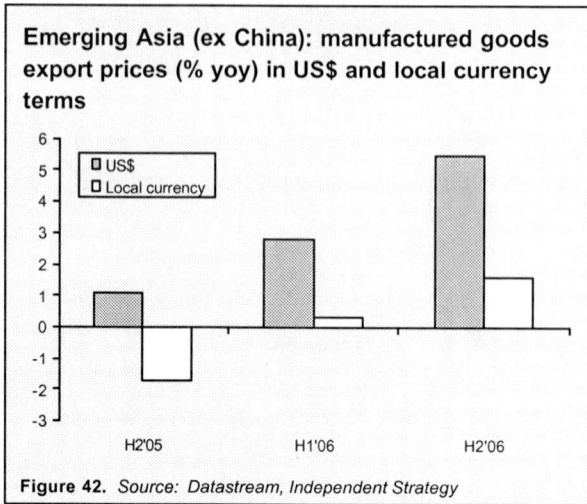

Figure 42. *Source: Datastream, Independent Strategy*

But a funny thing happens to Chinese goods on the way to the US market: price inflation disappears! The odd thing is that rising Asian export prices do not show up to nearly the same extent in US import prices. Normally, if there is a choice between US and Chinese statistics, we would choose the former — but not in this case.

The export price statistics from all Asian countries would have to be wrong for the US to be right. The old bugbears of Chinese transfer pricing, taxes and misreporting are unlikely to provide an alternative explanation to that of inflation because all the Asian exporters show a similar trend and would therefore have to be making similar errors.

But the main explanation for the continuing, albeit lessening, disinflationary impact of the prices of imports from Asia on the US is likely to be simply lags, made longer by the current global inventory cycle.

If this is true, then down the road, the supply of ever-cheaper goods, which is one of the major drivers of global disinflation and benefits of globalisation, will reverse. When that happens, there will be an impact on core inflation in the US and other OECD countries.

It may seem too much like chaos theory to predicate the earthquake of tightening global liquidity based upon the flapping of a butterfly's wings in the form of rising Chinese export prices. But stranger things have happened.

In a nutshell, it is the height of complacency to dismiss the market setbacks of May 2006 and of February 2007 merely as one-off events rapidly disposed of by markets. Both periods were rehearsals of what would happen to the global credit cycle if inflation were to rise (May 2006) or if the tide of yen liquidity were to reverse (February and July 2007) at the same time as global risk appetite fell (due to doubts about the US economy). We know now how serious either event could be if it happened big time. What we have seen so far are merely previews of the main feature. It is a matter of 'when' not 'if' the main movie hits the big screen.

Taking out insurance in the form of being long volatility, credit default swaps, equity puts and gold is a common sense approach to that dark day.

If the same economic scenario were to cause a sharp collapse in the dollar because the rest of the world narrows its growth gap with the US, that could perversely force up the cost of capital in the savings-starved US.

Bingo! Same result for asset markets. The US is the ultimate source of global liquidity. And under this scenario, interest rates would be rising in Japan too, so lessening capital outflows in search of higher yields.

The reduction of risk appetite

Risk, the main determinant of the liquidity multiplier, is also being grossly underpriced. Volatility measures for financial asset prices are close to their lows as Japanese banks and currency derivative markets continue to fund the yen carry trade (Figure 43).

And the pricing of 'tail risk' (the risk of a multi-standard deviation from the average pricing of a financial market or asset) remains supremely optimistic that such events won't happen.

REVERSING THE LIQUIDITY CYCLE

US VIX and volatility of Y/$ exchange rate

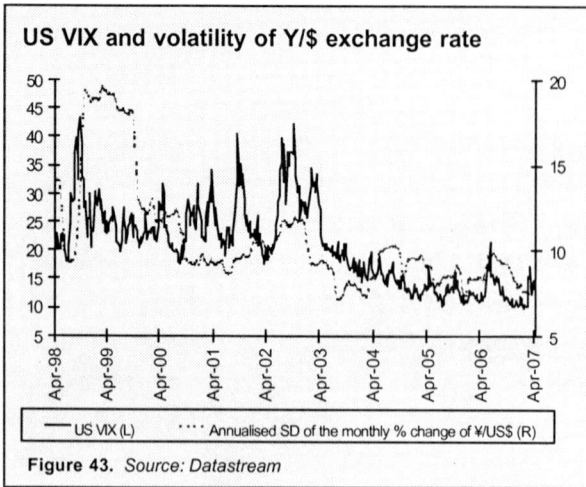

Figure 43. *Source: Datastream*

Markets are commensurately confident that the economic and credit cycle pose no threats. CDS rates, for example, are only a little higher than their cyclical lows. US and Euro banking sector willingness to lend is still at or close to boom readings.

Two things can be said about this. Random walk is back; markets believe the best forecast for tomorrow is yesterday (and all our yesterdays are of low volatility and disinflation). But, as Macbeth put it, "all our yesterdays have lighted fools the way to dusty death".

Second, there is a high degree of market confidence that extreme outcomes of any sort are highly improbable. All of this creates a circular logic: risk appetite contributes to financial market stability, which, in turn, boosts risk appetite that creates financial market stability.

But there is one really interesting thing about the lack of volatility that so many financial assets share: their price movements are becoming much more highly correlated as they become less volatile. This is like the uniform view of the aged arrayed upon serried ranks of deck chairs on a beach. When it comes to the time of dying they will all die at more or less the same time.

In sum, the current lack of volatility may contain much future volatility. And because diverse financial assets have seen their price movements become more closely correlated, there are few benefits of risk diversification to be expected when market turn sour. They will all fall together.

Nature (or human behaviour) won't follow Art (or the tranquility produced by financial engineering) so faithfully forever. In the end, humans are volatile and so is nature; every seventh wave is a big one and when it breaks, central bankers will be as King Canute, awash in a disobedient sea of their own undoing.

Reversals in the yen carry trade

In our vision the most likely exogenous shock that could cause the liquidity cycle to contract would be a reversal of the yen carry trade.

The yen currently supplies about 12% of global liquidity. Even a contraction of a few percentage points would have a substantial impact, particularly upon the smaller recipient markets of borrowed yen.

There are three risks for the yen carry trade: volatility in the price of the asset invested in with borrowed yen; volatility in the yen exchange rate versus the currency of that asset; and any closing of the gap between Japanese interest rates and the return on the asset purchased with borrowers' yen..

We can start by making life simple for ourselves. It is for the moment a very, very remote possibility that Japanese interest rates will rise to the level of those of say the US or New Zealand, or that the latter should fall to Japanese levels, for the foreseeable future. We can discount this risk.

That leaves us with two other risks: asset price and exchange rate volatility. A sharp rise in volatility in both, or either one, could wipe out the returns on borrowed yen and worsen anticipated returns per unit of risk (the Sharpe ratio).

REVERSING THE LIQUIDITY CYCLE

Nothing like this is happening now. The volatility of the yen exchange rate and global equity markets (as a proxy for destination assets of some yen borrowing) is very low and, if anything, trending down (Figure 44).

The return index based on borrowed yen and long US$, NZ$ and Euros has continued to trend higher while the standard deviation of those returns continues to trend lower. In other words the famous Sharpe ratio just gets better all the time. This is the very definition of a free financial lunch!

Geopolitics

Finally, political risk is rising. A political accident is waiting to happen. The villains are the Iranians, North Koreans and Islamic extremists. Their opportunity is a seriously weakened US. When a geopolitical accident does happen, I suspect it will be one with lasting economic costs. That could be the closing of the straits of Hormuz and a $100 oil price; a nuclear or germicidal terrorist attack that paralyses US logistics; or Kim Jong Il simply going completely off his rocker and nuking a neighbour. Global liquidity will contract viciously in nanoseconds despite the efforts of central bankers to kick-start the credit cycle by making money freely available.

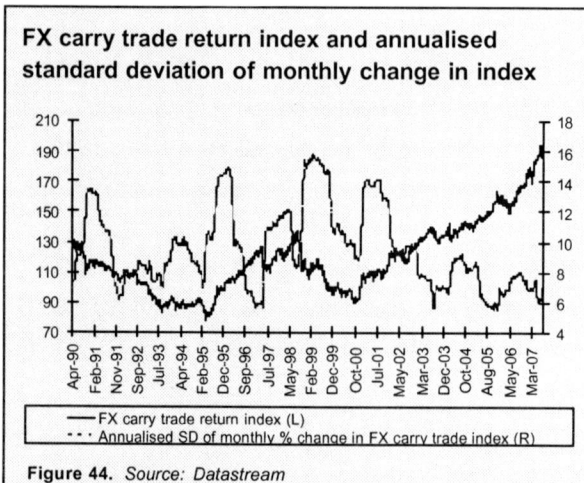

Wrapping it up

At the moment, liquidity is still growing faster than GDP, credit multipliers are intact, risk appetite remains solid and low volatility persists. These are the life blood of leverage and carry trades.

FX carry trade return index and annualised standard deviation of monthly change in index

— FX carry trade return index (L)
- - - Annualised SD of monthly % change in FX carry trade index (R)

Figure 44. *Source: Datastream*

But there are enough signs to worry. They may just be cracks in the concrete right now. But they could presage some uncomfortable plate shifts. The evidence is that there is some preliminary tightening of lending practices and reduction in risk appetite. And the yen carry trade is characterised by extreme valuation, high volumes and a shift in the attitude and awareness of officialdom to the consequences of a disorderly unwind. All may be symptomatic of a latter day bubble.

There are industry specific risks too. In leveraged buyout and private equity sectors, pro forma returns may be increasingly a function of cheap leverage than doing something fundamentally better with the acquired asset than under current ownership. And increasingly the exit sales of PE owned assets are to PE peers.

Can that other PE firm really hold a secret key to unlocking further value? Or has it simply got too much money to invest and too much leverage on offer not to use it? When similar things started to happen in the hedge fund industry, the years of big economic rents were already numbered.

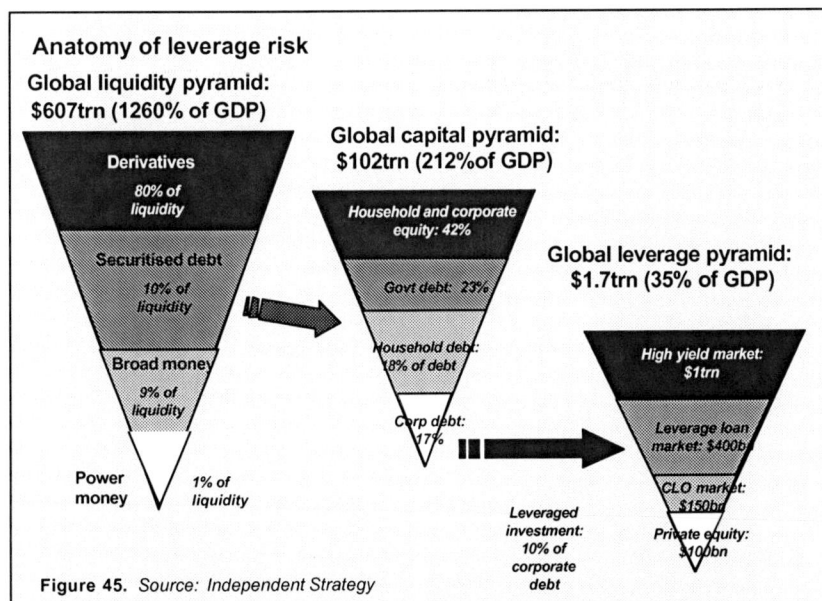

Anatomy of leverage risk

Global liquidity pyramid: $607trn (1260% of GDP)

Derivatives
80% of liquidity

Securitised debt
10% of liquidity

Broad money
9% of liquidity

Power money
1% of liquidity

Global capital pyramid: $102trn (212%of GDP)

Household and corporate equity: 42%

Govt debt: 23%

Household debt: 18% of debt

Corp debt: 17%

Leveraged investment: 10% of corporate debt

Global leverage pyramid: $1.7trn (35% of GDP)

High yield market: $1trn

Leverage loan market: $400bn

CLO market: $150bn

Private equity: $100bn

Figure 45. *Source: Independent Strategy*

REVERSING THE LIQUIDITY CYCLE

Leveraged borrowing is also under scrutiny by central bankers as a potential systemic risk and, being what it is, leveraged credit will shrink a lot when the liquidity cycle contracts even a little (Figure 45).

There is really no knowing when the liquidity party will end. Perhaps a sensible policy for most investment managers is to stay fairly fully invested, but to take out a lot of insurance in the form of going long volatility, gold, equity puts and credit default swaps.

Coconut Island —
New Monetarism on a desert island

There was this desert island that produced coconuts. The inhabitants ate them to survive. Any surplus they sold to passing boats, putting the money they got under their mattresses for a rainy day (very rare) and to buy luxuries and tools (from yet other passing boats).

Alas, the islanders never had enough money to find more water and plant more coconut trees. One day along came some gal in a pirogue who founded a bank. This was the Coconut Island's first bank. The bank paid interest on savings deposited with it. So everyone rushed to deposit their mattress money in the bank.

Before long, there were several banks, even some started by men. Together, they were able to lend far more money than the initial deposits. Every time they lent out money, a fairly high proportion ended up being redeposited back in the banks after being used to pay for more coconut trees, wells and houses. But there was a big change. The inhabitants were able to borrow enough from the banks to grow more trees and, later, to build proper houses for themselves.

Every coconut tree cost 100 widgits (w), including the land to grow it on and earned 8w a year. As the island had a government of sorts, there were taxes of 25%. Interest on borrowings was 4% and tax deductible. These were the only cash costs as everyone tended their own trees.

Most farmers started life with one palm tree. But since the advent of banks they could then borrow 100w to buy another. So an individual

Balance sheet (w)

	With banks		Before banks
Assets		**Assets**	
Palm trees X 2 =	200	Palm tree X 1 =	100
Liabilities		**Liabilities**	
Bank debt =	100	Bank Debt =	0
Equity =	100	Equity =	100
Total =	200	Total =	200

P&L account (w):

Revenues		**Revenues**	
Coconut sales	16	Coconut sales	8
Expenses		**Expenses**	
Interest at 4%:	4	Interest:	0
Pre-tax profit	12	Pre-tax profit	8
Tax at 25%:	3	Tax at 25%:	2
After-tax profit	9	After-tax profit	6

Figure 46. *Source: Independent Strategy*

farmer's balance sheet and profit and loss statement would look like Figure 46.

It was clear to all that the coming of the banks and the creation of credit had made everyone richer. Now everyone earned 9w a year. Previously, everyone in coconuts earned only 6w. And real productive capacity had doubled, as everyone now had two trees instead of one.

The along came some "smart" young people. People knew they were smart because they had calculating machines and dark glasses. People knew they were rich (and therefore smart) because they came in a speedboat.

They did not want to tend palm trees. In reality, the newcomers were beach bums. They intended to spend the day surfing and chatting up maidens in bars, which the island's new-found prosperity had made

possible, so increasing GDP, sexual disease, unwanted sprogs and unhappiness in one fell swoop. However, all of this cost money. The issue was how to get it.

The beach bums decided to buy 50% of one producer of palm trees. This would cost 60w as the farmer wanted to make more money than it had cost him to set up the business. And it would entitle the beach bums to the income of one of the two palm trees that the farmer would continue to tend as part of the deal.

Balance sheet (w)

Assets
50% of 1 Coconut enterprise =   60

Liabilities
Bank debt   50
Equity   10
Total   60

The P&L looked like this:
Revenues
Coconut sales   8
Expenses
Interest at 4%   2

Pre-tax profit   6
Tax at 25%   1.5
After-tax profit   4.5
Return on equity (4.5w/10w = 45%)

Figure 47. *Source: Independent Strategy*

Then the beach bums went to one of the banks and borrowed 50w and put down 10w of their own money and called their new company PCE, standing for the Private (Coconut) Equity Fund. The PCE balance sheet would now look like Figure 47.

Everyone lived happily afterwards. The beach bums earned a 45% return on their equity. The farmer still earned a good living and had an extra 60w to play with. And he still earned a net 2w from his remaining palm tree (revenues 8w less interest 4w and tax 2w = 2w).

Then along came another set of beach bums, in a chopper this time, with much the same ambitions as their peers. Alas, there were no more coconut

COCONUT ISLAND

Balance sheet (w)	
Assets	
Loans (50% of the banks' outstanding loans of 150)	75
Liabilities	
Bank debt	67.5
Equity	7.5
Total	75
The P&L looked like this:	
Revenues	
Interest income (75 at 4%)	3
Expenses	
Interest (67.5 at 0.25%)	0.2
Pre-tax profit	2.8
Tax at 25%	0.7
After-tax profit	2.1
Return on equity (2.1w/7.5w = 28%)	

Figure 48. *Source: Independent Strategy*

enterprises for sale (everyone was hanging out for higher prices after the first deal became known).

But they had a new idea. Instead of buying a coconut enterprise, the new beach bums took themselves off to the bank and said "we want to buy half of your loan book (=150w, of which 100w are for loans to palm tree owners and 50w to PCE) at book value".

The bank manager thought this was a good idea because he could use the new money to make more loans, this time for home finance that paid 7% instead of 4%. And anyway, he didn't like the coconut business so much any more and wanted to diversify his loan book. Moreover, he could lend the new set of beach bums 90% of the cost of the loan book they were buying, which he offered at 3% — the current short-term bank rate.

But the beach bums were international players and they said 'no thanks' to the loan by the local bank. Instead, they rang their Japanese bank (although none of them was Japanese). The Japanese bank lent them the money based on Japanese market rates currently standing at 0.25% for three years. The rate of interest was adjustable quarterly. But the beach bums didn't worry about the variable interest rate as they could lock in that rate for three years by buying interest-rate options (derivatives).

So the second set of beach bums were happy and set up a company called CCDO, standing for Collateralised Coconut Debt Obligations. Their financial statements read happily too as in Figure 48.

The second set of beach bums were happy. They earned a 28% return on their equity. The banker was happy. He was able to lend an extra 75w for housing (which caused the islands real estate to rise in prices by 25% in the following months). This not only diversified his business, but increased the average interest yield on his loan book from 4% to 5.5%. His gross interest income (upon which his bonus was based) jumped by 37.5% (from 6w to 8.25w).

The island's people were happy because they felt, and were, richer. House prices soared. Foreign yen inflows had made the widget strong. So everyone could afford a holiday in Miami. In fact, people felt so good that they started to put less money aside for a rainy day. After all, why should they save? Rising asset prices meant that their houses and palm trees kept making them richer while they slept. And the government was happy because it made lots more tax from increased profits and real estate taxes.

So everyone was happy, except for one old guy who lived on the beach and owned no home and no palm tree. He pointed out that only the original loan had created real wealth by doubling coconut capacity in which it was invested. All the rest was just a layering of debt on an unchanged productive asset. He drew a T account

---

Balance sheet (w)

Assets

2 x Palm trees	200

Liabilities	292.5

(original bank debt 100w + PCE debt 50w + CCDO debt 67.5w + housing debt 75w)

Net worth	(92.5)

Figure 49. *Source: Independent Strategy*

in the sand. He said it represented the real balance sheet of the island, as in Figure 49.

So he said to those who would listen: " you may feel rich. But it is only asset price inflation and debt that makes you think so. Instead you are bankrupt. Because even your houses are worthless if the trees stop producing nuts". But then the happy blue tide rose and the rippling waters washed away his writing and any trace of concern in the mind of his audience...

Until one horrible day, when the price of coconuts fell 25% and the bank doubled the cost of lending because no-one was saving any more and inflation had reached 5%, meaning it had to charge 7% on all loans. You can work the balance sheets backwards yourself to see they do not balance any more!

Bibliography

Bank of International Settlements, Quarterly reviews, *www.bis.org*

Bank of International Settlements, *The global OTC derivatives market, end December 2006*

IMF, World Economic Outlooks, *www.imf.org*

IMF, Global financial stability bi-annuals, *www.imf.org*

International Swaps and Derivatives Association, *www.isda.org*

US Comptroller of the Currency, *www.occ.treas.gov*

US Comptroller of the Currency, quarterly derivatives fact sheets, *www.occ.treas.gov/deriv/deriv.htm*

Federal Bank of New York, Current issues in economics and finance, December 2006, (Matthew Higgins, Thomas Klitgaard and Robert Lerman), *Recycling petrodollars; www.newyorkfed.org*

Federal Reserve Bank, *www.federalreserve.gov*

Ben S. Bernanke, Homer Jones Lecture, 14 April 2005: *The global saving glut and the US current account deficit, www.federalreserve.gov/boarddocs/speeches/2005/20050414/ default.htm*

Ben S. Bernanke, Brian P. Sack, and Vincent R. Reinhart, Brookings Papers on Economic Analysis (2004), *Monetary Policy Alternatives at the Zero Bound: An Empirical Assessment; www.brook.edu*

Hernando de Soto, *The mystery of capital,* Bantam Press, 2000

Claudio Borio and Philip Lowe, BIS Working paper No 114, July 2002, *Asset prices, financial and monetary stability: exploring the nexus*

William White, BIS working paper 205, April 2006: *Is price stability enough?*

Michael Bordo, IMF World Economic Outlook, April 2003, p64 Box 2.1: *When bubbles burst*

Kunio Okina and Shigenori Shiratsuka, Monetary and Economic Studies, Institute for Monetary and Economic Studies, Bank of Japan, vol. 20(3), pages 35-76, October 2002, *Asset price bubbles, price stability and monetary policy: Japan's experience*

Robert Shiller, *www.econ.yale.edu/~shiller/*

James Tobin, Journal of Money Credit and Banking, Vol 1No 1 pp 15-29Tobin J. (1969) A general equilibrium approach to monetary theory

Andrew Smithers and Stephen Wright, *Valuing Wall street: protecting wealth in turbuluent markets* McGraw-Hill, 2000

Charles Kindleberger, *Manias, panics and crashes — a history of financial crashes,* 2000

Hyman Minsky, in Kindleberger and Laffargue, editors: *Financial Crises,* 1982; *The financial-instability hypothesis: capitalist processes and the behaviour of the economy*

Printed in the United Kingdom
by Lightning Source UK Ltd.
132354UK00002B/183/A